UX Writing and Intuitive Design Processes in a Nutshell

Quick and Easy UX writing crash course for Busy People

What's Inside?

Introduction

Have you ever found yourself navigating through software or an app? The words you see on the screen that guide you or tell you what to do – that's UX writing. It's like the storyteller making sure you get where you want to go without getting lost. UX writing, or User Experience writing, is the strategic use of language to enhance and guide users through digital interfaces. It's the thoughtful crafting of words within a product or service to ensure a seamless and intuitive user experience. UX writers collaborate with designers, developers, and other stakeholders to create clear, concise, and user-centric content that helps in navigation, comprehension, and overall satisfaction.

What UX Is and What It Is Not

UX is like the overall vibe of your whole experience with something – be it a game, an app, or a website. It's not just about the looks; it's about how everything feels and works together. UX, or User Experience, is the holistic impression a person has when interacting with a product, system, or service. It encompasses everything from usability and accessibility to emotions and aesthetics. It's not just about making things look good; it's about making them work well and feel right.

UX is not just the visual design or the user interface (UI). While UI is a crucial aspect of UX, it's only a part of the whole picture.

UX involves understanding users, their needs, and their pain points, then designing and optimizing the entire experience accordingly.

What Does UX Writing Do?

1. **Helps You Understand:** UX writing makes sure you know what's going on. It's like a helpful friend giving you directions so you don't end up in the wrong place.

Example: Instead of saying *"Error 404,"* it might say, *"Whoops, it seems like we took a wrong turn. Let's get back on track!"*

2. **Talks the Same Way Everywhere:** It keeps things consistent. Imagine if your favorite game suddenly started talking in a completely different language – confusing, right? UX writing keeps everything sounding familiar.

Example: If the app says *"Next"* in one place, it won't say *"Continue"* somewhere else for the same thing.

3. **Understands Your Feelings:** UX writing knows how you might feel and talks to you in a way that makes you feel good. It's like a buddy who gets you.

Example: Instead of saying *"Invalid input,"* it might say, *"Oops, something went wrong. Mind trying that again?"*

4. **Keeps It Simple:** It makes things easy to understand. Nobody likes reading a super long paragraph just to do something simple.

Example: Instead of saying, *"Your session has expired. Please log in again,"* it might say, *"Uh-oh, you've been away for a bit. Time to log in again!"*

5. **Fixes Mistakes Nicely:** When you mess up, it doesn't scold you. It's like a coach helping you get back on track.

Example: Instead of saying **"Invalid password,"** it might say, *"Oops, the password doesn't match. Give it another shot!"*

6. **Includes Everyone:** It makes sure everyone feels welcome and not left out. It's like making a party where everyone feels invited.

Example: Instead of saying *"Hey guys,"* it might say, *"Hey everyone!"* to include everyone, no matter who they are.

So, UX writing is basically the friendly guide in a digital product, either an app or software, that makes sure everything is smooth and enjoyable for you. It's like having a friend who helps you out, providing useful directions on how to navigate a digital product.

Difference between UX Writing and Copywriting

UX writing is like your tech-savvy buddy. It's the words that help you navigate and understand stuff in apps or games. It's all about making your digital experience smooth and fun. Copywriting on the other hand, is like the smooth talker. It's the words that convince you to do something – buy a cool gadget, click a link, or sign up for something awesome. It's the persuasive language that makes you go, "Yeah, I want that!"

Example: If you see an ad saying, *"Get the hottest game now and level up your gaming experience!"* – that's copywriting trying to make you excited to grab the game. Here are some notable differences:

1. Purpose

UX Writing Focuses on enhancing user experience by providing clear, concise, and helpful text within a product or interface. It guides users through tasks and helps them understand how to interact with a digital product. Example: Error message in a form - *"Please enter a valid email address."*

Copywriting aims to persuade and sell by creating compelling and engaging content. It's often used in marketing materials, advertisements, and promotional campaigns. Example: Ad headline - *"Unleash Your Adventure: Explore the World with Our Travel Gear!"*

2. User-Centered vs. Brand-Centered

UX Writing puts the user first. It's about making the user's journey seamless´ and intuitive. It focuses on clarity and simplicity, ensuring users can easily navigate and understand the interface. Example: Button label - *"Continue"* instead of *"Next Step."*

Copywriting highlights the brand's personality and value proposition. It aims to evoke emotions and create a connection between the audience and the brand. Example: Brand tagline - *"Empowering Your Success Every Step of the Way."*

3. Length and Tone

UX Writing is typically short and to the point. Aims for clarity and usability. Avoids unnecessary information. Example: Loading message - *"Hang tight. We're preparing your experience."*

Copywriting can be longer and more expressive. Uses a tone that aligns with the brand's personality and the emotions the brand wants to evoke. Example: Product description - *"Indulge in the rich, velvety taste of our decadent chocolate, crafted with love for your moments of pure bliss."*

4. Context

UX Writing is embedded within the user interface, providing guidance and feedback during specific interactions. Example: Tooltip - *"Hover over the icon for more information."*

Copywriting appears in marketing collateral, advertisements, and promotional materials where the goal is to capture attention and persuade. Example: Social media ad caption - *"Transform your mornings with our energizing coffee blends. Wake up to a new you!"*

Understanding copywriting can be challenging sometimes. It often incorporates humor, puns, quotes, sarcasm, and reverse psychology, which might not be immediately clear. Therefore, a key distinction between UX writing and copywriting lies in their perspectives: UX treats users solely as users, not customers.

Criteria for Good UX Writing

Having understood the definition of UX writing and its distinctions from copywriting, let's now examine the attributes that define effective UX writing. When crafting microcopy for websites or social media, it's essential to adhere to a set of straightforward rules. A fundamental guideline dictates that quality UX writing should encompass six key components. These components are:

1. The information must be Necessary
2. It must be Clear
3. It must be Concise
4. It must be Useful
5. It must be conversational
6. It must be Branded

Necessary UX Writing

When you're whipping up microcopy, it's tempting to get all fancy with jokes or out-of-the-box stuff. But here's the golden rule: make sure your words and elements are actually needed. "Necessary" means they should be like superheroes solving problems. Whether it's words, design, or a combo, they've got to answer your clients' burning questions.

Why stick to the essentials? Well, going overboard with long or unnecessary stuff can mess with your audience's brain, confusing them and making them swipe left on your product. Take a 404 error page, for example – it tells users a page took a hike and points them in a new direction. And that success message? It's like a virtual high-five, letting users know their moves were top-notch. Keep it necessary

let's consider a practical example of necessary UX writing for a password reset feature:

Unnecessary Version: *"Oops! Looks like something went wrong. Please bear with us as we try to fix it. In the meantime, feel free to explore other parts of our site. We appreciate your patience!"*

Necessary Version: *"Forgot your password? No worries! Enter your email below, and we'll send you a secure link to reset it. Easy peasy!"*

In the necessary version, the text is concise, clear, and directly guides the user on how to resolve their issue. It focuses on providing a solution without unnecessary information, reducing cognitive load, and enhancing the overall user experience.

Clear UX Writing

Clear UX writing ensures that the language used is straightforward, simple, and easily understood by the target audience. It avoids jargon, overly complex sentences, and ambiguity. The goal is to convey information in a way that users can quickly grasp without confusion. Clear UX writing takes into account the diverse needs of users, including those with varying levels of literacy, language proficiency, or cultural backgrounds. It strives to create an inclusive experience by using language that resonates with a broad audience. Unnecessary complexity can hinder user understanding and engagement. Clear UX writing advocates for simplicity, cutting out unnecessary information and presenting only what is essential for users to achieve their goals.

Unclear Version: *"Operation Successful! Your data has been received. Thank you for your submission."*

Clear UX Writing: *"Hooray! Your message has been sent. We'll get back to you within 24 hours. Thanks for reaching out!"*

In the clear version, the message is concise, positive, and provides specific information about what the user can expect next. It avoids unnecessary technical terms and communicates the successful submission in a friendly and reassuring tone. This kind of clarity helps users understand the status of their action and sets clear expectations for the next steps, contributing to a positive user experience.

Concise UX Writing

Crafting microcopy can be a bit of a journey, and it's easy to end up with wordy paragraphs that tell a story before getting to the main point. The issue? Too many words become a chore for users, demanding more brainpower than they're willing to give. When instructions get too lengthy, users might lose interest and bail on the app or tech product. That's why it's crucial to keep things short and sweet. Conciseness lets users:

- Glide through the product effortlessly
- Swiftly grasp the most important info
- Elevate their overall experience
- Trim down cognitive load with simple words and short sentences, making skimming a breeze.

Unclear Version: *"Please create a password that is at least 8 characters long, includes a mix of uppercase and lowercase letters, at least one number, and a special character."*

Concise UX Writing: *"Create a strong password: 8+ characters, mix of uppercase/lowercase, at least 1 number, and a special character."*

In the concise version, unnecessary details are trimmed, and the essential requirements are presented clearly. This makes it easier for users to quickly understand what is expected, promoting a smoother and more efficient user experience during the password creation process.

Useful UX Writing
What turns a piece of writing into a useful guide?

It's pretty straightforward.

A useful copy delivers just the right amount of info for users to smoothly continue their journey without any headaches. This often involves suggesting the next steps when things get tricky, offering comfort when they hit a snag, or motivating and nudging them in the right direction.

Why does usefulness matter in UX writing?

- It keeps users engaged with the app, website, or product.
- It offers a reassuring sense of security, letting users know everything's okay.
- It guides users to achieve their goals by providing helpful direction.

Unhelpful Version: *"Error 404: Page not found."*

Useful UX Writing: *"Oops! It looks like the page took a wrong turn. No worries, though! Click the 'Back' button or try our homepage to keep the journey going."*

In the useful version, the message not only communicates the error but also provides guidance on what the user can do next. It acknowledges the issue, offers a solution, and maintains a reassuring tone, encouraging users to continue exploring the website without feeling frustrated. This kind of UX writing enhances the user experience by turning a potential roadblock into a helpful redirection.

Conversational UX Writing

For our UX writing to hit the sweet spot of clarity, brevity, and user-friendliness, it's got to be conversational. But what does that really mean? It's all about giving our copy a natural, non-techy, and empathetic voice – one that sounds human and not robotic.

Why bother with this chatty style, you ask?

Well, because it makes the writing human, captivating, and downright welcoming. Users find it easier to chat with the product when the language feels natural and gets their struggles. It's like talking to a friend who gets it.

Non-Conversational Version: *"No tasks found. Click 'Add Task' to create a new task."*

Conversational UX Writing: *"Whoa, looks like your to-do list is taking a breather! Ready to give it some action? Hit 'Add Task' to get the ball rolling!"*

In the conversational version, the tone is friendly, with a touch of personality. It acknowledges the situation in a lighthearted manner and encourages the user to take action. This creates a more engaging and approachable user experience, making the interaction feel less robotic and more like a friendly conversation.

Branded UX Writing

Branded UX writing is a content strategy that marries language and messaging to craft a distinctive and unified user experience tailored to a specific brand. This approach blends the worlds of branding and user experience (UX) design, focusing on shaping language that aligns seamlessly with a brand's personality, voice, and tone. The ultimate aim? Forge a user experience that feels not just seamless but uniquely personal, engaging, and consistent across every interaction point.

Why does branded UX writing matter? Here are a few key reasons:

1. **Consistency:** Branded UX writing ensures that messaging maintains a consistent vibe across all touchpoints, spanning websites, mobile apps, social media, and various digital platforms.
2. **Differentiation:** It helps a brand carve its own niche by creating a distinct personality and voice that sets it apart from competitors, resonating uniquely with users.
3. **Engagement:** Branded UX writing has the power to transform a user's journey into something more captivating and memorable, enticing them to return and connect with the brand on a deeper level.
4. **Accessibility:** By employing clear, concise, and easily understandable language, branded UX writing makes

content more accessible to a broader audience, enhancing overall inclusivity.

Generic Version: *"Congratulations! You've completed today's workout. Click here for more details."*

Branded UX Writing: *"Boom! High five, champion! You crushed today's workout. Want to dive deeper into your progress? Hit that button for all the juicy details!"*

In the branded version, the language is infused with energy and positive reinforcement, aligning with the brand's persona as a motivating fitness companion. The tone is celebratory, creating a distinct and engaging experience for the user. This approach not only delivers information but also reinforces the brand's personality and encourages the user to feel a sense of accomplishment.

Elements Of UX Writing

UX writing is typically applicable in the development of digital products such as apps, software, websites, social media platforms and other products that require users to either use the product online or offline on their computer or phones. UX writing is also applicable to electronic, automobiles, and other forms of technology. Basically there are a few elements that are fairly consistent with digital products, and they are:

1. CTAs (Call to Action)
2. Place Holders
3. Success messages
4. Password Errors
5. Empty States
6. 404 Error pages

How CTAs Work

CTA is short for "call to action," It is the final line of action on a website or app nudging you to do something specific, like "Sign up now" or "Buy now." These CTAs play a crucial role in UX writing by directing users toward a particular goal.

Let's break down what makes a good CTA:

- **Clear and Simple Language:** Good CTAs use straightforward words, making it crystal clear what happens when you click. For instance, "Add to cart" beats "Purchase item."
- **Active Voice:** Keep it lively! Good CTAs use active voice, making it obvious that the user is the one taking action. "Start your free trial" is more lively than "Free trial starting now."
- **Easy to Spot:** Don't play hide-and-seek! Good CTAs are front and center, easy to find on the page. They stand out and practically wave at the user.
- **Consistent Design:** Keep it classy! Good CTAs maintain the same look throughout the website or app, so users always recognize them.

Here are the rules of using CTAs:

1. **Action-Oriented Language:** Your CTA should use words that spur the user to act – like "start," "join," or "subscribe."
2. **Be Specific:** Don't beat around the bush. A good CTA clearly states what happens when you click. "Start your free trial" beats "Get started."
3. **Create Urgency:** Light a fire! Use language that makes users feel like they need to act now. "Limited time offer" or "Only 3 spots left" can do the trick.
4. **Keep it Short and Sweet:** No novels, please! A good CTA is concise – ideally, a button is 3 words max, and links are 5 to 6 words, depending on the situation.

5. **Choose Verbs:** When in doubt, use action words. If there are no objects, throw in an adverb. For example, "Subscribe for free" or "Sign up immediately."
6. **Prioritize Clarity:** Don't be too clever. A good CTA prioritizes clear communication over being daring or funny. "Get a surprise" might confuse; "Sign up for a treat" is clearer.

What's the difference between good and bad CTAs?

Good CTAs:

−   Clear, concise, and easy to understand.
−   Active voice and action-oriented.
−   Consistent design, prominently displayed.

Bad CTAs:

−   Confusing, unclear, or hard to find.
−   May use passive voice or unclear language.
−   Design may blend in, making it tough to spot.

When in doubt, keep it clear, keep it simple, and make it easy for users to say, "Yes, I'll click that!"

Join Twitter today.

Full name

Phone or Email

Password

☑ Tailor Twitter based on my recent website visits. Learn more.

Sign up

Understanding Place Holders

Placeholders succinct phrases or words strategically inserted into form fields and other interface elements to guide users on the type of information required. Here are the types of Placeholders:

1. Instructional Placeholders:

These are like signposts, guiding users. For example, in a name field, the placeholder could say: *"Enter your full name."*

2. Example Placeholders:

Think of these as samples. In a phone number field, an example placeholder might be: *"(555) 555-5555."*

3. Combination Placeholders:

The best of both worlds, providing guidance and an example. For an email field: *"Enter your email address (e.g., example@email.com)."*

Things to Keep in Mind

- **Keep it Short:** Make placeholders brief. Long ones can be a bit overwhelming.
- **Plain Language:** Use words anyone can understand. Skip the tech talk.
- **Format for Visibility:** Make them stand out with simple formatting, like bold or italics.
- **Ask Questions or Prompt:** Turn placeholders into friendly prompts. Instead of a plain "Enter date," try "When's the event? MM/DD/YYYY."
- **User Test:** Before finalizing, see how real users react. Do they get it? Are they finding it easy?
- **Date Details:** Especially for dates, add a little flair. Instead of just "MM/DD/YYYY," try "Select event date: MM/DD/YYYY."

Instagram

wongmjane

real_password_hunter2_plz_dont_steal

Log In

Forgot your login details? **Get help signing in.**

Log In as @wongmjane

OR

Don't have an account? **Sign up.**

Creating Success Messages

Success messages in UX writing are short and clear notifications displayed in digital interfaces. They confirm to users that a particular action or task has been successfully completed. These messages are designed to provide immediate feedback, assuring users that their interactions with the system were effective and achieved the intended goals.

Types of Success Messages

- **Confirmation Messages:** These are straightforward acknowledgments that confirm the completion of an action. For example, after submitting a form: *"Your form has been successfully submitted."*
- **Validation Messages:** When users input information, validation messages assure them that the provided data is accurate and meets the required criteria. A classic example is a password change success message: *"Your password has been updated successfully."*
- **Progress Messages:** These keep users in the loop during lengthier processes. For instance, during a file upload: *"Uploading... 75% complete."*
- **Gratitude Messages:** Expressing gratitude adds a personal touch. After a purchase, for instance: *"Thank you for your order! Your payment was successful."*

Rules to Follow When Crafting Success Messages

- **Clarity is King:** Keep it crystal clear. Users should instantly understand what they've accomplished.
- **Positive Language:** Use positive and encouraging language. Celebrate the user's success with phrases like "Congratulations" or "Well done."
- **Be Specific:** Specify what was achieved. Vague messages can leave users uncertain. Instead of "Success!" say "Your account has been created successfully."

- **Relevance to User's Action:** Tie the message directly to the user's action. If they subscribed to a newsletter, say, "You're now subscribed. Welcome to our community!"
- **Avoid Jargon:** Steer clear of technical jargon. Success messages are not the place for confusing terms.
- **Consistency Across Platform:** Maintain consistency in tone and style across your platform. Whether it's a website or a mobile app, users should feel a cohesive experience.
- **Visual Distinction:** Make success messages visually distinct. Use color, icons, or placement to ensure they stand out.
- **User Testing:** Test success messages with real users to ensure they resonate positively and effectively communicate the intended message.

By adhering to these rules, success messages become a central component of a positive user experience, reinforcing user confidence and satisfaction.

Passwords Error Messages

When users fumble with their passwords on an online platform, an error message pops up, politely informing them that their password combo missed the mark. This is what we call a password error message.

As a UX writer, these messages are a crucial part of creating a smooth user experience. They're the digital bouncer, ensuring only the right folks get into the password-protected party. The messages we encounter before and after entering our passwords form what we call the password error system. It's a big deal in UX because it shapes how users feel and whether they'll stick around.

Reasons for Using Password Errors

- **Creating Secure Passwords:** They guide users in crafting passwords that shield their personal info from cyber threats.
- **Preventing Lockouts:** By catching incorrect entries, they prevent users from accidentally getting locked out of their accounts.
- **Reducing Support Requests:** They help cut down on the flood of support calls from users who forgot their passwords or are wrestling with login gremlins.

Functions of Password Errors

- **Creating Strong Passwords:** They signal the strength of a new password based on criteria like length, complexity, and uniqueness.
- **Blocking Incorrect Entries:** By pinpointing mistakes and offering suggestions, they stop users from accidentally inputting the wrong passwords.
- **Boosting Security:** They enforce security measures, like requiring numbers, symbols, or a mix of uppercase and lowercase letters.

Types of Password Errors

- **Passwords Do Not Match:** Example: *"The passwords you entered do not match. Please try again."*
- **Password Too Short:** Example: *"Password must be at least 8 characters long. Please choose a longer password."*
- **Weak Password:** Example: *"Password is too weak. Include a combo of letters, numbers, and symbols for a stronger password."*
- **Passwords Don't Match (Confirmation):** Example: Displayed when the user enters different passwords in *'password'* and *'confirm password'* fields.

Things to Keep in Mind When Crafting Password Error Messages

- **Be Clear and Concise:** Use simple, jargon-free language. Keep it short and sweet.
- **Provide Actionable Solutions:** Guide users on what to do next – reset the password, contact support, or check email for recovery instructions.
- **Avoid Blaming the User:** Focus on solutions, not blame. Suggest using a password manager or creating a stronger password.
- **Provide Reassurance:** Assure users that their data is safe and the issue can be resolved quickly.
- **Use Visuals and Animations:** Employ icons or animations to help users identify and understand the problem, making the recovery process more user-friendly.

User-Friendly Empty States

Empty States in UX writing refer to the messaging and visuals that appear on a screen when a user encounters an empty or blank state, such as a search result page with no outcomes or a new user who hasn't added any data. Essentially, it's the content that guides users on what steps to take next to begin interacting with the app or website.

Types of Empty States

- **Placeholder Empty States:** These are default states that appear when users first access a screen or interface, often displaying a generic message like "No data available."
- **Error Empty States:** These states appear when there's a problem with the application, such as a broken link or network error.
- **User-Generated Empty States:** Created by users when they delete content or cancel a process.

Rules for Creating Empty States

- **Clarity and Conciseness:** Clearly convey the message in a concise manner. For instance, avoid long-winded explanations and opt for straightforward language like *"No content available."*

- **Provide Actionable Guidance:** Offer clear directions on what users can do to remedy the empty state. For example, include a call-to-action (CTA) suggesting users "Add New Content" or "Start Exploring."
- **Maintain Consistency:** Keep language and design elements consistent across all empty states to create a cohesive user experience. Consistency helps users navigate seamlessly.
- **Engagement Elements:** Make the empty state engaging to keep users interested, even when there's no content. Consider using light humor or subtle animations.
- **Relevance to Context:** Ensure the empty state aligns with the context of the application. The content should be relevant to the user's journey within the app or website.

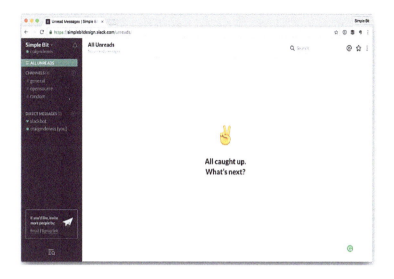

Drafting 404 Errors Pages

A 404 error page in UX writing is a standard HTTP response code indicating that the server did not find the requested page. In simpler terms, it's the "Page Not Found" message users encounter when trying to access a URL that doesn't exist or has been moved.

Types of 404 Error Pages:

Standard 404 Page: The generic "Page Not Found" message.

"404 - Page Not Found. The page you're looking for might have been removed or doesn't exist."

Humorous 404 Page: Injecting humor to soften the frustration of not finding the page.

"404 - Oops! This page seems to be on vacation. Maybe it's sipping a tropical drink on a beach somewhere."

Search-Integrated 404 Page: Offering a search bar to help users find what they were looking for.

"404 - We couldn't find the page you wanted. How about searching for it?"

Rules for Creating 404 Error Pages

- **Clear Messaging:** Use straightforward language to explain the error. Avoid technical jargon.
- **Provide Navigation:** Include links to the homepage or popular sections to guide users back.
- **Maintain Branding:** Keep the design and tone consistent with the overall brand for a cohesive experience.
- **Engagement Elements:** Consider adding engaging visuals or messages to alleviate frustration.
- **Helpful Suggestions:** Offer suggestions or popular links to direct users to relevant content.

Multiple Variations of 404 Error Pages

Interactive 404 Page: Includes interactive elements like games or quizzes to entertain users.

"404 - Lost in cyberspace? Play a quick game while we find your page!"

Custom Illustration 404 Page: Features a custom illustration to convey a sense of personality.

Example: A cute robot holding a sign saying, *"404 - Looks like I took a wrong turn. Let's get you back on track!"*

Apology 404 Page: Includes a brief apology for the inconvenience.

"404 - Oops! We're sorry. The page you requested seems to have taken a detour."

In creating 404 error pages, the goal is to turn a potential frustration into a positive or, at the very least, a less frustrating experience. Clear communication, navigation options, and a touch of creativity can transform a disappointing error into a moment of engagement for users.

Other HTTP Status Codes

There are several HTTP status codes used to indicate the outcome of a client's request to a server when interacting with a web page. Each status code conveys a specific meaning about the success, redirection, or error of the request. Here are some common HTTP status codes:

200 OK: This status code indicates that the request was successful, and the server has returned the requested data. After submitting a form, the user receives a success message confirming that their data has been successfully submitted.

"Success! Your form has been submitted. Thanks for your input!"

201 Created

It signifies that the request has been fulfilled, resulting in the creation of a new resource. It means that upon signing up for a new account, the user is redirected to a welcome page, confirming the successful creation of their account.

"Congratulations! Your account has been successfully created. Welcome aboard!"

204 No Content

The server successfully processed the request but there is no additional content to send in the response. After updating their profile picture, the user receives a notification that the update was successful, but no additional content is displayed.

"Update complete! Your profile picture has been updated successfully."

400 Bad Request: This status code indicates that the server could not understand the request due to malformed syntax or other client-side errors, Implying that the user attempts to submit a form with missing required fields, and the system displays an error message highlighting the missing information.

"Oops! It seems you missed some required fields. Please fill them out and try again."

401 Unauthorized: It means that authentication is required and has failed, or the user does not have the necessary permissions. That means a user tries to access a secure part of the website without logging in, and the system prompts them to log in or create an account.

"Access Denied! Please log in or create an account to view this page."

403 Forbidden: The server understood the request, but it refuses to authorize it. The client does not have permission to access the requested resource. Meaning a user attempts to access an admin-only section without the necessary permissions and is presented with a message indicating restricted access.

"Restricted Access! You do not have the necessary permissions to view this content."

500 Internal Server Error: This is a generic error message indicating that the server has encountered an unexpected condition that prevented it from fulfilling the request. While completing an online purchase, the user encounters a generic error message apologizing for technical difficulties and encouraging them to try again later.

"Technical Difficulties! We apologize for the inconvenience. Please try your purchase again later."

502 Bad Gateway: The server, while acting as a gateway or proxy, received an invalid response from an upstream server it accessed in attempting to fulfill the request. The user is browsing a website, and a temporary glitch occurs due to issues with the server. The system displays an error message with a suggestion to refresh the page.

"Hiccup in the Connection! Something went wrong on our end. Try refreshing or come back shortly."

503 Service Unavailable: The server is not ready to handle the request. Common causes include temporary overloading or maintenance of the server. Meaning the website is undergoing maintenance, and users attempting to access it are greeted with a message indicating that the service is temporarily unavailable but will be back soon.

"Maintenance Mode! We're sprucing things up. The service will be back online soon. Thank you for your patience."

These codes help both developers and users understand the outcome of their interactions with a website or web application. They play a crucial role in communication between the client (user's browser) and the server, ensuring a clear understanding of the status of each request.

Voice and Tone in UX Writing

The voice is the distinct personality and style that a brand uses to communicate with users. It's like the brand's unique way of speaking—consistent across all interactions, from error messages to welcome prompts. Think of it as the character of your brand coming through in the words you choose. Mailchimp has a friendly and approachable voice, using casual language. For example, *"Nice work! Your campaign is ready to send."*

Tone, on the other hand, is the mood or attitude that the voice takes in a particular situation. It can change while keeping the overall voice intact. Imagine your brand as a person – the voice is who they are, and the tone is how they express themselves in different situations.

Slack maintains a professional yet friendly voice throughout. *"You're all caught up!"* when there are no new messages. In an error situation, it might say, *"Whoops! Looks like something went wrong. Our team is on it."*

Why Brands Need a Distinctive UX Writing Voice

Having a distinctive voice in UX writing helps brands in several ways:

- **Consistency:** It creates a consistent experience, making users feel like they're interacting with the same entity across the entire platform.
- **Brand Personality:** It gives the brand a personality, making it more relatable and memorable.
- **User Trust:** A familiar voice builds trust. Users know what to expect and feel more comfortable.
- **Differentiation:** It sets the brand apart from competitors, making it instantly recognizable.

Step-by-Step Strategy to Define UX Writing Voice

- **Know Your Audience:** Understand who your users are. What language resonates with them? Tailor your voice to speak directly to your audience.
- **Define Brand Attributes:** Identify the key attributes of your brand. Is it playful, professional, or innovative? Translate these attributes into words.
- **Analyze Competitors:** Check out what your competitors are doing. How can you sound unique? Find a gap and fill it with your brand voice.

- **Create a Style Guide:** Develop a style guide that outlines your voice and tone. Include examples to show your team how to apply them in different scenarios.
- **Test and Iterate:** Test your voice with real users. Get feedback and be ready to tweak it based on what works best.
- **Reflect Brand Values:** Ensure your voice aligns with your brand's core values. If your brand is eco-friendly, your voice could reflect sustainability and care for the environment.
- **Be Authentic:** Don't try to be something you're not. If humor suits your brand, inject it naturally. Authenticity builds trust.
- **Flexibility for Tone:** Define a range of tones that fit different scenarios. Your brand can be friendly in a success message and more serious in an error message.

Remember, defining your UX writing voice is an ongoing process. Keep adapting it based on user feedback, brand evolution, and the ever-changing digital landscape. It's your brand's way of saying, "Hey, we're here, and we get you!"

Let's explore the diverse voices and tones of various business brands in the US:

Mailchimp:

- Voice: Friendly and conversational.
- Tone: Encouraging and upbeat.

Example: *"Great news! Your campaign is ready to roll. Time to shine!"*

Slack:

- Voice: Professional yet approachable.
- Tone: Supportive and understanding.

Example: *"You're all caught up! Need a hand with anything?"*

Airbnb:

- Voice: Warm and welcoming.
- Tone: Personal and inclusive.

Example: *"Welcome to your home away from home! Explore and make memories."*

Taco Bell:

- Voice: Playful and youthful.
- Tone: Fun and irreverent.

Example: *"Crunchwrap Supreme - because your taste buds deserve a party!"*

IBM:

- Voice: Professional and authoritative.
- Tone: Informative and innovative.

Example: *"Explore the latest advancements in AI technology with IBM Watson."*

Nike:

- Voice: Inspirational and empowering.
- Tone: Motivational and confident.

Example: *"Just do it. Your journey starts with that first step."*

Coca-Cola:

- Voice: Nostalgic and uplifting.
- Tone: Celebratory and joyful.

Example: *"Share a Coke and a smile – spreading happiness, one sip at a time."*

Zappos:

- Voice: Customer-focused and friendly.
- Tone: Helpful and conversational.

Example: *"Need assistance? Our Zappos team is here 24/7 to make your shopping experience seamless."*

Harley-Davidson:

- Voice: Rebel and authentic.
- Tone: Freedom and adventure.

Example: *"Ride free. Live authentic. Explore the open road with Harley-Davidson."*

Target:

- Voice: Accessible and family-friendly.
- Tone: Welcoming and community-oriented.

Example: *"More than a store, we're your neighborhood Target – where quality meets affordability."*

These examples showcase the versatility in brand voices and tones. Each brand crafts its unique identity to connect with its audience, conveying not just products or services, but a distinctive personality and values.

Designing Your Style Guide

Think of a UX Writing Style Guide as the go-to handbook for your brand's way with words. It's a detailed document that lays down the rules, preferences, and personality quirks of your brand's language. This guide ensures that every piece of writing, from error messages to product descriptions, sounds like it's coming from the same friendly voice.

Why Do We Need a UX Writing Style Guide?

Consistency is King: Imagine if every button had a different label or every error message sounded like it was from a different universe. Chaos, right? A style guide brings order, making sure your brand talks the same talk everywhere.

Building Brand Personality: Your brand has a personality, and the way you talk should reflect that. A style guide is your brand's personality map, helping you maintain a consistent tone that resonates with your users.

Guiding the Team: Whether it's a seasoned UX writer or a newbie joining the team, a style guide is like a mentor. It guides the team on the do's and don'ts, ensuring everyone's on the same page (pun intended).

Contents of a UX Writing Style Guide

Voice and Tone: If your brand's voice is like a friendly neighbor, your tone might be empathetic in error messages and celebratory in success messages.

Grammar and Punctuation: Do you prefer the Oxford comma? Are contractions encouraged? The style guide settles these debates.

Word Choices: Should you say "buy now" or "get it today"? The style guide helps you make consistent choices.

Formatting Guidelines: Are headings in sentence case or title case? Does your brand prefer bold or italics for emphasis? The style guide keeps it crystal clear.

Examples for Common Scenarios: "If a user forgets their password, use a reassuring tone like 'No worries! Let's get you back in.'"

Inclusive Language: Guide on using language that's inclusive and respectful to diverse audiences. For instance, *"Welcome everyone"* instead of *"Welcome guys."*

User Interface (UI) Copy Guidelines: Specify how buttons, tooltips, and form fields should be labeled. For instance, "Submit" instead of "Go" for a form submission button.

Consistent Terminology: Decide on the terms you use. Is it "shopping cart" or "basket"? The style guide ensures everyone's singing from the same dictionary.

Dos and Don'ts: "Do use contractions to sound conversational. Don't use jargon that might confuse users."

Review and Update Procedures: Set a schedule for reviewing and updating the style guide. Language evolves, and your guide should keep up.

Remember, your style guide is your brand's language compass. It's not a rulebook to stifle creativity but a roadmap to keep everyone, including future recruits, heading in the same linguistic direction.

How to Write your Style Guide

Creating your own style guide for UX writing doesn't have to be a labyrinthine task. Follow these 5 straightforward steps to craft a guide that keeps your team on the same linguistic voyage:

1. Do Your Planning:

- Define your target audience: Who are you speaking to? Understand your users' needs and preferences.
- Brainstorm your content: Let the ideas flow. What messages does your brand want to convey?
- Create a comprehensive project plan: Plot out the journey. What steps will you take to bring your style guide to life?

2. Research and Gather Your Information:

- Consult your organization's voice and tone guidelines: What does your brand sound like? Ensure your guide aligns.
- Interview your target audiences: What do they find helpful? Tailor your content to their needs.

- Interview important stakeholders: Get insights from colleagues, bosses, and your team.
- Cluster your target audience's needs: Prioritize. What's most crucial for your users?
- Adjust your project plan accordingly: Be flexible. Adapt your plan based on your findings.

3. Define All Contributors:

- Get in touch with content managers, freelancers, and writers: Ensure everyone's on the same linguistic ship.
- Plan according to contributors' availability: Coordinate efforts. Align the plan with everyone's schedule.
- Keep clearance in mind: Understand your organization's approval process. Know if content needs the green light from legal or communication departments.

4. Choose Your Medium:

- Research how other companies publish their style guides: Explore different options. Learn from the navigational choices of other companies.
- Research the most commonly used media in your organization: Where do your team members frequent? Choose a medium they're comfortable with.
- Liaise with teams responsible for the chosen medium: Ensure a smooth integration. Collaborate with the teams handling the chosen platform.

5. Write and Test Your Style Guide:

- Plan and schedule your writing time: Break it down. Set realistic timelines for each writing phase.
- Write a draft and improve it with other writers: Collaborate. Seek input from your team to refine the guide.
- Test your draft using feedback collected: Iterate. Use user feedback to enhance your guide.
- Repeat the process for upcoming sessions: Keep refining. Each session brings a chance to improve.

As a final tip, adhere to technical writing quality criteria. Your UX style guide should tell your audience how things work. So, ensure clarity and precision in your language.

Sample of a UX Writing Style Guide

Here's the structure for creating a real life style guide. Remember that your style guide is very flexible and can contain whatever you want it to. This particular style guide is for a fictional Brand called *"Silly Goose"* This brand owns a large digital online learning platform for kids with learning disorders.

Silly Goose Writing Style Guide 2024

Table of Contents

Introduction

- Purpose of the Style Guide
- Target Audience

Brand Overview

- Voice and Tone
- Brand Voice
- Tone Variations
    - o Encouraging Tone
    - o Supportive Tone
    - o Celebratory Tone

Grammar and Punctuation

- Consistency in Grammar
- Punctuation Standards
- Use of Contractions

Word Choices

- Preferred Terms
- Inclusive Language Guidelines
- Clarity and Simplicity

Formatting Guidelines

- Headings and Subheadings

- Use of Bold and Italics
- Lists and Bullet Points

Examples for Common Scenarios

- Error Messages
- Success Messages
- CTAs and Prompts

Inclusive Language

- Guidelines for Inclusive Language
- Examples of Inclusive Phrasing
- Pronoun Usage

UI Copy Guidelines

- Labeling Buttons and CTAs
- Tooltip Usage
- Form Field Instructions

Consistent Terminology

- Glossary of Terms
- Preferred Vocabulary

Dos and Don'ts

- Dos for Positive User Experience
- Don'ts to Avoid Confusion

Review and Update Procedures

- Schedule for Regular Reviews
- Process for Updating the Style Guide

Medium Selection

- Options for Publishing
- Integration with Learning Platforms
- Collaboration with Development Teams

Writing and Testing Process

- Planning Writing Time
- Collaborative Drafting
- Testing with User Feedback
- Iterative Improvement Process

This style guide is a living document designed to maintain consistency and clarity in all communications across Silly Goose. As we strive to create an inclusive and supportive online learning environment, let this guide be our compass in crafting a positive user experience for children with learning disorders.

Introduction to Accessible UX Writing

Accessibility in UX writing refers to creating content that ensures all users, regardless of their abilities or disabilities, can easily understand, navigate, and interact with digital products. It's about breaking down barriers and making information universally available and comprehensible.

Why Do We Need Accessible UX Writing?

1. **Inclusivity:** Accessible UX writing ensures that everyone, regardless of their abilities, can access and benefit from digital content. It promotes an inclusive online experience.
2. **Comprehension:** Clear and concise language helps users understand information easily. Accessible UX writing removes ambiguity and enhances comprehension for all users.
3. **Navigational Support:** Well-crafted UX writing provides clear instructions and guidance, assisting users in navigating through digital interfaces seamlessly.
4. **Legal Compliance:** Many regions have legal requirements for accessibility to ensure equal access. Accessible UX writing helps organizations comply with these regulations.

5. **User Satisfaction:** When users can easily understand and interact with digital content, it leads to higher satisfaction and a positive user experience.

Examples of Accessible UX Writing

Alt Text for Images:

- Non-Accessible: *"Image123.jpg"*
- Accessible: *"A happy group of students studying together."*

Clear Error Messages:

- Non-Accessible: *"Error: Invalid Input"*
- Accessible: *"Oops! It looks like there's an issue with the information you entered. Please double-check and try again."*

Simplified Language:

- Non-Accessible: *"Utilize the navigation bar to access additional features."*
- Accessible: *"Use the menu to find more options."*

Text-to-Speech Friendly Content:

- Non-Accessible: Complex sentences with jargon.
- Accessible: *"Our learning tools help kids of all ages. Click for more info."*

Well-Structured Headings:

Non-Accessible: No clear hierarchy in headings.

Accessible: *"Lesson 1: Introduction | Lesson 2: Practice Exercises | Lesson 3: Final Assessment"*

Keyboard Navigation Instructions:

- Non-Accessible: Assumes mouse usage.
- Accessible: *"Use the Tab key to navigate and Enter to select."*

Contrast for Readability:

- Non-Accessible: Low contrast between text and background.
- Accessible: High-contrast text for easy readability.

Embracing Diversity, Abilities, and User Experience

Understanding the full scope of user abilities becomes a complex task due to the diverse nature of users. Users, with their unique capacities, interact with products in ways that suit them best.

Let's consider a few examples of factors that might pose challenges:

- **Visual Impairment:** Conditions like color blindness pose challenges.
- **Auditory Impairment:** Users with hearing difficulties need thoughtful design.
- **Motor/Mobility Issues:** Considerations for hand movement constraints.

Exploring Neurodiversity

Neurodiversity recognizes the natural differences in human brains. Even though our brain structures are similar, our abilities and focus levels vary widely. UX writers are attuned to these variations, accommodating users with diverse needs. Here are some examples associated with neurodiversity:

- **Dyslexia:** Challenges in reading and interpreting written text.
- **Attention Deficit Hyperactivity Disorder (ADHD):** Variations in attention span and focus.
- **Autism:** Differing social and communication preferences.
- **Dyscalculia:** Difficulty in comprehending and working with numbers.
- **Mental Health Issues:** Factors impacting mental well-being.

Understanding and addressing this spectrum of diversities ensures a more inclusive and user-friendly experience for all.

Defining On-Screen Texts

On-screen texts refer to any written content that appears on a digital display, such as computer monitors, mobile screens, or other electronic devices. These texts encompass a wide range of information, including body content, navigation labels, buttons, form fields, error messages, and more.

In the digital field, on-screen texts play a very important role in communicating information, guiding users through interfaces, and facilitating interactions within websites, applications, and software.

Rules for Creating On-Screen Texts in UX Writing

Clear and Readable Fonts: Choose fonts that are easily readable, avoiding overly decorative styles.

Example: Opt for Arial or Helvetica for body text.

Adequate Font Size: Maintain a minimum font size (e.g., 16 pixels) for optimal legibility.

Example: Set body text at 16 pixels for comfortable reading.

Contrast for Visibility: Ensure sufficient contrast between text and background.

Example: Use dark text on a light background or vice versa.

Consistent Text Styling: Maintain consistent font styles, colors, and formatting.

Example: Use the same font and color for similar types of information.

Descriptive Hyperlinks: Make hyperlink text descriptive, indicating the destination or action.

Example: Instead of "Click Here," use "Read more about our services."

Alt Text for Images: Provide descriptive alt text for images to convey content or function.

Example: Alt text for a product image: "Latest smartphone model in silver."

Simplified Language: Use clear and straightforward language, avoiding unnecessary complexity.

Example: Instead of "utilize," use "use" for simplicity.

Avoiding All Caps: Refrain from using all capital letters for entire sentences or paragraphs

Example: Use "Product Features" instead of "PRODUCT FEATURES."

Line Length and Spacing: Optimize line length and spacing to prevent visual strain.

Example: Keep lines at a comfortable length, and add spacing between paragraphs.

Keyboard Accessibility: Ensure users can navigate and interact with on-screen text using a keyboard.

Example: Provide clear instructions for keyboard shortcuts or navigation.

Using Alt Texts

Define alt texts. What is the purpose of alt texts? Where should you add alt texts? How should you write alt texts? Provide examples for right and wrong ways. Use clear terms. Provide examples where necessary.

Alt texts, short for alternative texts, are descriptive text alternatives added to images, graphics, or other non-text elements within digital content. These texts serve a crucial role in making web content accessible to individuals with visual impairments or those using screen readers. Alt texts provide a textual description of the visual content, ensuring that users with disabilities can comprehend and engage with the information presented.

Purpose of Alt Texts:

- **Accessibility:** Enable individuals with visual impairments to understand the content.
- **SEO Enhancement:** Improve search engine optimization by providing context to image content.

Where to Add Alt Texts:

- **Images:** Photos, illustrations, or graphics.
- **Buttons:** Describing the action or purpose.
- **Icons:** Conveying the meaning or function.

How to Write Alt Texts

- **Be Descriptive:** Clearly describe the content or function of the image.
- **Concise Language:** Keep it succinct while conveying essential information.
- **Avoid Redundancy:** Don't repeat information already present in the surrounding text.

Examples:

Right Way: Image of a Beach Sunset: *"Vibrant sunset over the ocean, casting a warm glow on the sandy beach."*

Wrong Way: Image of a Beach Sunset: *"Image123.jpg"* (Uninformative and redundant).

Right Way: Button with Shopping Cart Icon: *"Add to Cart"* (Describes the action).

Wrong Way: Button with Shopping Cart Icon: *"Button123"* (Lacks context or purpose).

Right Way: Educational Icon: *"Illustration of a graduation cap for educational resources"* (Describes the icon's meaning).

Wrong Way: Educational Icon: *"Icon123"* (Doesn't convey the icon's purpose).

By following these guidelines, alt texts contribute significantly to creating an inclusive digital experience, ensuring that all users, regardless of their abilities, can fully engage with and comprehend the content.

UX Writing Documentation

In UX writing, there's a phase where we gather, write down, save, and handle information – we call it the documentation phase. Here's the thing: UX writers usually don't hear much about these steps. But guess what? That's changing right now.

We're going to take a look at how to jot down your UX words, what tools to use for the documentation process, and why it's super important. Imagine putting all your written stuff in one spot so your developer, designer, translators, and the whole team can easily grab it.

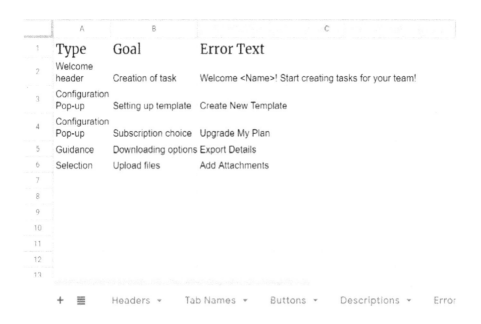

Type	Goal	Error Text
Welcome header	Creation of task	Welcome <Name>! Start creating tasks for your team!
Configuration Pop-up	Setting up template	Create New Template
Configuration Pop-up	Subscription choice	Upgrade My Plan
Guidance	Downloading options	Export Details
Selection	Upload files	Add Attachments

Headers ▾   Tab Names ▾   Buttons ▾   Descriptions ▾   Error

Choosing the Right Way to Document

When deciding how to document your work, there are a few important things to consider:

Efficiency: Choose a method that doesn't take up too much time. If it's too complicated or time-consuming, people might not want to use it. A quick and easy documentation process is more likely to be embraced by your team.

Accessibility and Sharing: Make sure the documentation is easy to access and share with everyone involved. Accessibility is crucial for effective collaboration. Use a platform that allows easy sharing and access, ensuring all team members can contribute.

Adaptability: The chosen method should be flexible enough to meet the specific requirements of each project. Different projects may have different needs, so your documentation method should be adaptable.

Translation Capability: If your product is used by people who speak different languages, ensure your documentation method supports translations. Consider a documentation tool that easily integrates translations for a global audience.

Visual Context: Include visual elements, like screenshots, to provide context alongside the text. Use a platform that allows you to add images to your documentation for better understanding.

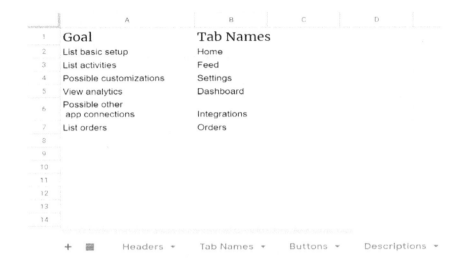

	A	B	C	D
1	**Goal**	**Tab Names**		
2	List basic setup	Home		
3	List activities	Feed		
4	Possible customizations	Settings		
5	View analytics	Dashboard		
6	Possible other app connections	Integrations		
7	List orders	Orders		
8				
9				
10				
11				
12				
13				
14				

+ ≡   Headers ▾   Tab Names ▾   Buttons ▾   Descriptions ▾

What to Document

There are two main types of text that need documentation:

On-Screen Text: This includes all the words users see on the interface, such as buttons, labels, and instructions. Examples are Microcopy like button labels, marketing texts, onboarding instructions, and legal copy.

Alt Text: This is text describing visual elements like icons or images for users who rely on screen readers. For examples, descriptions of non-decorative icons and explanations for images

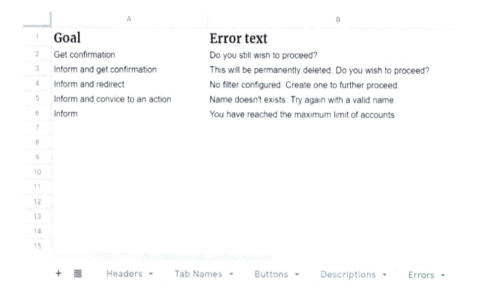

	A	B
1	**Goal**	**Error text**
2	Get confirmation	Do you still wish to proceed?
3	Inform and get confirmation	This will be permanently deleted. Do you wish to proceed?
4	Inform and redirect	No filter configured. Create one to further proceed.
5	Inform and convice to an action	Name doesn't exists. Try again with a valid name.
6	Inform	You have reached the maximum limit of accounts
7		
8		
9		
10		
11		
12		
13		
14		
15		

+ ▦   Headers ▾   Tab Names ▾   Buttons ▾   Descriptions ▾   Errors ▾

How to Prepare UX Writing Documentation

Follow these five simple steps to get your documentation ready:

- **Understand Project Requirements:** Ask questions like how many languages the product needs to be translated into and who will be providing text input.

- **Identify Stakeholders:** Engage with designers, developers, product owners, legal, and marketing teams to understand their specific needs.

- **Choose the Right Tool:** Consider factors like cost, the number of users, and whether the tool meets stakeholder needs. For instance, Pick a tool that aligns with everyone's requirements.

- **Set Up Your Tool:** Customize the tool to match your workflow, such as setting categories, tags, and naming conventions.
- **Test with Stakeholders:** Conduct a limited test with a subset of screens and involve stakeholders to gather feedback for improvement.

Here is a list of tools for documenting your UX writing:

Confluence: Confluence is a collaboration tool that allows teams to create, share, and collaborate on documents. It integrates seamlessly with Jira and other Atlassian products, providing a comprehensive solution for project management and documentation.

Google Docs: A cloud-based document editor that enables real-time collaboration. It's easy to use, accessible from anywhere, and offers robust collaboration features.

Notion: Notion is an all-in-one workspace that allows teams to create documents, wikis, and databases. It is flexible and customizable, with the ability to integrate various types of content in one place.

Airtable: A cloud-based spreadsheet and database tool with collaboration features. It allows for the creation of custom databases, making it suitable for organizing and documenting content.

Turtl: Turtl is a secure, collaborative platform for organizing and sharing notes and documents. It focuses on security, ensuring that sensitive information is protected while still providing collaborative features.

UXPin: UXPin is a design and collaboration platform that allows teams to create prototypes and document design decisions. It integrates design and documentation, making it suitable for teams focused on UX design.

Quip: A collaboration platform that combines documents, spreadsheets, and chat in one interface. It facilitates real-time collaboration and integrates with Salesforce for seamless project management.

Slack: A messaging platform for teams, which can also be used for collaborative document sharing. Provides instant communication, with the ability to share documents and get quick feedback.

Miro: Miro is a collaborative online whiteboard platform that supports visual documentation and ideation. It is ideal for teams that need a visual approach to document workflows, user journeys, and design concepts.

Basecamp: Basecamp is a project management and team collaboration tool that includes document sharing features. It simplifies project management and offers a centralized place for documentation.

Figma: This tool is a collaborative interface design tool that supports the creation of design documents. It is perfect for real-time collaboration on design files, making it suitable for teams working on UI/UX.

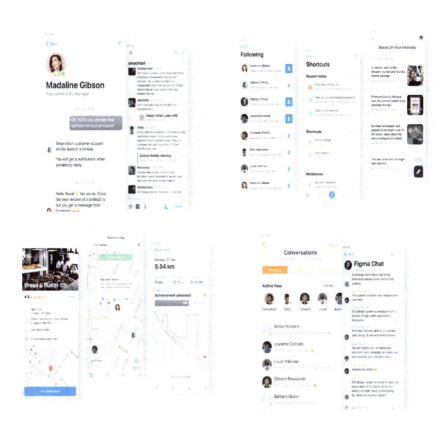

Evernote: Evernote is a note-taking app that allows users to organize and share their notes. It provides multi-platform support, easy organization, and quick sharing of documentation.

GitBook: GitBook is a documentation platform that integrates with Git for version control. It has Version history tracking, making it suitable for projects where documentation changes need to be closely monitored.

Markdown: A lightweight markup language that is easy to write and read. It contains Simple syntax, widely supported, and compatible with various platforms and tools.

Storybook: This is a tool for developing UI components in isolation and documenting them. It streamlines the development and documentation of UI components, enhancing collaboration between designers and developers.

Remember to assess your team's specific needs and preferences when selecting a tool for documenting UX writing. Each tool has its own strengths, and the best choice depends on factors such as collaboration requirements, design focus, and overall project management preferences.

Incorporating UX Writing In Agile Projects

Agile is a project management and product development approach that prioritizes flexibility, collaboration, and responsiveness to change. In agile projects, the development process is broken down into small increments, with cross-functional teams working in short, iterative cycles called sprints. The goal is to deliver a functional product quickly, gather feedback, and make adjustments as needed. Agile emphasizes customer satisfaction, adaptability, and continuous improvement.

Integration of UX Writing into Agile Processes

Integrating UX writing into agile processes is crucial for several reasons:

User-Centric Focus: Agile aims to create products that meet user needs, and UX writing is integral to the user experience. Integrating UX writing ensures that the language and communication within the product align with user expectations and preferences. For instance, clear and concise UX writing in interface elements, such as buttons and labels, enhances user understanding and satisfaction.

Collaboration Across Disciplines: Agile relies on cross-functional collaboration, involving designers, developers, and other team members. Including UX writers in the agile team ensures that content considerations are addressed early and consistently throughout development. Collaborating on user stories and design mockups allows UX writers to provide input on language choices and user interactions.

Iterative Improvement: Agile projects iterate quickly, allowing for continuous improvement based on user feedback. Integrating UX writing ensures that content can be refined and adjusted in response to user testing and evolving project requirements. Adapting UX writing based on user feedback during each sprint leads to a more user-friendly and polished final product.

Early User Validation: Agile encourages regular user testing and validation. Integrating UX writing means that content can be tested early in the development process, reducing the risk of major usability issues later on. Testing different variations of microcopy helps identify the most effective language for guiding users through the interface.

Consistent User Experience: Consistency is a key agile principle. Integrating UX writing ensures a consistent tone, terminology, and messaging throughout the product, enhancing the overall user experience. A consistent voice in error messages and tooltips contributes to a cohesive and understandable user interface.

Efficient Communication: Agile teams rely on efficient communication. Integrating UX writing streamlines communication between team members by providing clear guidelines on language and content. Clear documentation for UX writing helps developers implement the desired language without confusion.

Phases of Agile Design processes in UX Writing

The Agile design process in UX writing typically involves several phases, each with its own set of activities and objectives. Here are the key phases in the Agile design process for UX writing:

1. Discovery Phase

- Understand the project goals, user needs, and business requirements.
- Collaborate with stakeholders to gather project information.
- Conduct user research to understand the target audience and their expectations.
- Define user personas and identify key user journeys.

2. Planning Phase

- Develop a plan for UX writing tasks within the Agile framework.
- Break down the project into user stories and tasks.
- Collaborate with the team to estimate the effort required for each task.
- Prioritize tasks based on user needs and project goals.

3. Design Phase

- Create content that aligns with the project requirements and enhances the user experience.
- Collaborate with designers to ensure alignment between content and visual elements.
- Write and iterate on microcopy for interface elements such as buttons, labels, and tooltips.

- Create onboarding and instructional content to guide users through the product.

4. Development Phase

- Implement the UX writing content within the development cycle.
- Work closely with developers to integrate the written content into the user interface.
- Provide support and clarification on any content-related questions during implementation.
- Collaborate on user acceptance testing (UAT) to ensure content works as intended in the live environment.

5. Testing Phase

- Evaluate the effectiveness of UX writing through user testing and feedback.
- Conduct usability testing to gather feedback on the clarity and effectiveness of the written content.
- Iterate on the content based on user feedback and testing results.
- Ensure consistency and alignment with the overall user experience.

6. Deployment Phase

- Release the product or features to users based on the Agile development cycles.
- Collaborate with the team to finalize and deploy the product.
- Monitor user interactions and feedback after deployment.
- Address any post-launch issues related to UX writing.

7. Retrospective Phase

- Reflect on the Agile design process to identify areas for improvement.
- Conduct a retrospective meeting with the team to discuss what worked well and areas for improvement.
- Document lessons learned for future projects.
- Iterate on processes and workflows to enhance efficiency in subsequent iterations.

Kanban Board in UX Writing

A Kanban board is a visual project management tool used to optimize workflow, manage tasks, and visualize the status of work items. In the context of UX writing, a Kanban board helps streamline the content creation process, providing a clear visual representation of tasks, their progress, and priorities. The board typically consists of columns representing different stages of the workflow, and tasks (or user stories) move from one column to the next as they progress.

Key Columns in a UX Writing Kanban Board

To-Do: Tasks that are identified and ready for UX writing.

In Progress: Tasks actively being worked on by the UX writers.

Review: Tasks completed by UX writers and awaiting review from stakeholders or other team members.

Testing/Feedback: Tasks that have undergone initial reviews and are now being tested or waiting for feedback.

Done: Completed tasks that have been finalized, tested, and approved.

KANBAN BOARD

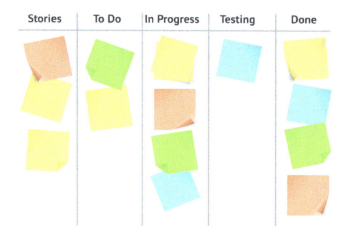

Stories	To Do	In Progress	Testing	Done

Benefits of a Kanban Board in UX Writing

- Provides a clear and visual representation of the workflow, making it easy to track progress and identify bottlenecks.
- Allows teams to prioritize tasks and focus on the most critical UX writing elements first.
- Facilitates collaboration by providing a shared space where team members can see and understand the status of each task.
- Supports continuous improvement by allowing teams to identify areas for optimization and streamline their processes.
- Adaptable to changing priorities and requirements, making it well-suited for Agile and iterative development methodologies.

Tools that Provide Kanban Boards for UX Writing

Trello: This online tool is a popular project management tool that uses boards, lists, and cards to organize tasks. It provides simple and intuitive interface, easy collaboration, and integration with various third-party tools.

Jira: Jira was developed by Atlassian, is a comprehensive project management and issue tracking tool. Provides powerful customization, integration with other Atlassian products, and widely used in Agile development.

Asana: This tool is a versatile project management tool that offers various views, including Kanban boards. It provides User-friendly, supports task dependencies, and integrates with many third-party applications.

Monday.com: This is a work operating system that includes visual project management features. It provides customizable boards, timeline views, and collaboration features for cross-functional teams.

ClickUp: This tool is an all-in-one project management platform that allows teams to customize their workflows. Offers flexibility, features rich customization options, and supports Agile methodologies.

Notion: It is an all-in-one workspace that allows teams to create documents, databases, and boards. It is Flexible and customizable, allowing teams to adapt the Kanban board to their specific needs.

ZenHub: This tool is a project management solution that integrates directly with GitHub for software development teams. It provides seamless integration with GitHub, providing a Kanban-style interface for managing GitHub issues.

When choosing a tool for a UX writing Kanban board, it's important to consider factors such as team preferences, integration capabilities, and the specific features required to support the UX writing workflow.

User Research in UX Writing

User research is like investigating to understand the people who will use a product or service. It's about studying what they need and what troubles them so that designers can create products that work exceptionally well for them.

So, how does this user research connect with UX writing? Well, in writing for user experience, the first thing is looking closely at what users need and what problems they face. So, when writers are putting words together (copy), they have the best understanding of what users want and need.

Types of User Research

1. Qualitative Research

It's about collecting and understanding non-numerical information, like ideas, opinions, or experiences. Instead of counting things, you're trying to figure out why people feel a certain way about a product.

2. Quantitative Research

This one deals with numbers—collecting and analyzing numerical data to find patterns or test ideas. Counting how many people use a feature and trying to see if there's a connection between that and their satisfaction.

3. Primary Research

Doing your own research, going out and collecting information directly, for instance, conducting surveys or interviews yourself to gather specific details.

4. Secondary Research

Using information that others have already collected. For example, reading reports or studies done by other people to get information.

UX Writing Research Categories

I. **Exploratory Research:** Looking deeply into a subject to get a better understanding, usually before starting a big project. Example, trying to figure out what users might need before designing a new feature.

II. **Validating Research:** Collecting and analyzing data to check if certain ideas or concepts are right, for instance, testing a new feature with users to see if it actually solves the problem it's supposed to.

III. **Research Methods in UX Writing**

IV. **Competitor Analysis:** Checking out what others are doing in the same space. Also seeing how other similar products or websites write and present information.

V. **Conversation Mining/Analysis:** Looking at what people are saying about a product online. Reading comments on social media to understand what users are talking about.

VI. **Target Group Observation:** Watching how the specific group you're interested in behaves. Observing how teenagers use a new app to see what they like and dislike.

VII. **Focus Groups:** Bringing a small group of people together to discuss a product or service. Also, having a group discussion with users about a new website design.

VIII. **User Interviews:** This includes talking directly to users to get their thoughts and opinions. And asking people questions about their experience with a mobile app to gather insights.

Explanatory Research in UX Writing

Explanatory research means digging deeper to understand why users do what they do. It's about going beyond just knowing their needs; it's understanding the reasons behind those needs, behaviors, and feelings. In simpler terms, it's like asking "why" to get a better picture of what users want and why they want it.

Importance of Explanatory Research

It's crucial because it helps writers not only identify user needs but also grasp the underlying reasons behind those needs. This deeper understanding allows for more effective communication through writing. If you know why users feel a certain way or why they prefer a particular feature, you can create content that resonates better with them.

Difference between Exploratory Research and Explanatory Research

Exploratory Research: Its purpose is to explore and understand a subject before starting a project. It looks at the broad landscape to find inspiration and insights. For instance, trying to gather ideas about what users might need before designing a new feature.

Explanatory Research: It explains the "why" behind user behaviors or needs. It delves deeper into specific aspects to understand the reasons behind certain user actions. For example, instead of just knowing that users want a simpler interface, explanatory research seeks to understand why simplicity is important to them—whether it's because they're new users, or they prefer a quick and easy experience.

Preparation Process for User Research

Step 1: Define Your Goal

Clearly understand what you want to learn from the research. If you're designing a new app, your goal might be to find out how users currently handle similar tasks and what challenges they face.

Step 2: Identify Your Target Users

Figure out who will use your product or service. If your app is for students, your target users are likely to be students of different ages and backgrounds.

Step 3: Choose Your Research Methods

Decide how you'll gather information—interviews, surveys, or observing users in action. If you're making a website, you might choose to talk to users and watch them navigate through similar websites or a prototype.

Step 4: Create Your Research Questions

Develop questions that will help you get the information you need. Instead of asking, "Do you like this feature?" you might ask, "How do you usually complete this task, and what problems do you encounter?"

Step 5: Plan Your Approach

Outline the details of your research plan, like where and how you'll conduct interviews or surveys. If you're doing interviews, decide if it'll be in person, on the phone, or online, and schedule time accordingly.

Step 6: Recruit Participants

Find people who fit your target user group and are willing to participate. If your app is for young professionals, reach out to them through social media or local groups.

Step 7: Conduct the Research

Carry out your plan, whether it's talking to people, watching them use your product, or collecting survey responses. If you're doing interviews, ask your questions and listen carefully to what users say.

Step 8: Analyze the Data

Look at the information you gathered and find patterns or common themes. If many users mention the same difficulty, like a confusing menu, that's a pattern to pay attention to.

Step 9: Draw Insights

Understand what your data is telling you about your users' needs and behaviors. If users struggle with a specific feature, it suggests that improving or simplifying it could enhance their experience.

Step 10: Share Findings and Take Action

Communicate what you've learned with your team and decide on the next steps. If users love a particular aspect, consider highlighting it more in your product, and if they find something confusing, think about how to make it clearer.

Competitor Analysis in Research

Competitor analysis is like taking a peek at what other companies or products are saying and how they're saying it. It's a way to understand what works well in the world of words, and what doesn't, so that when you're writing for your own product or service, you can do it even better.

Why is Competitor Analysis Important in UX Writing?

Learning from Others: It's like checking out what your friends are doing before starting a project. You might get some cool ideas from them!

Avoiding Mistakes: Imagine your friends tried something, and it didn't work out so well, you can learn from that and avoid making the same mistakes.

Standing Out: If everyone in your workplace wears the same shirt, you might want to wear something different to stand out. Competitor analysis helps you find your unique style.

Understanding User Expectations: It's like knowing what games everyone likes to play before suggesting a new game. If people are used to a certain way of writing, you can match that or add a little twist to surprise them.

Steps in Competitor Analysis

1. **Identify Competitors:** Make a list of friends who are doing something similar to what you're doing.
2. **Explore Their Content:** Read what they've written. See how they explain things and the words they use.
3. **Look for Strengths and Weaknesses:** Find out what your friends are really good at and where they might be struggling.
4. **Note the Tone and Style:** Think of it like noticing if your friends are funny, serious, or somewhere in between. It helps you understand what style people like.
5. **Check User Reactions**: Look at comments or reviews to see how people react to what your friends are doing. What do they love, and what do they wish was better?

Benefits of Competitor Analysis in UX Writing

- **Inspiration for Your Writing:** It's like getting ideas for your school project by looking at what others have done.
- **Avoiding Repetition:** You don't want to say the exact same thing as your friends, right? Competitor analysis helps you find your own words.
- **Connecting with Users:** By knowing what people like from others, you can make sure your writing connects well with them.
- **Continuous Improvement:** Just like practicing a game to get better, regularly looking at what others are doing helps you improve your writing skills.

Conversation Mining in User Research

Conversation mining, in straightforward terms, is a method that combines both qualitative and quantitative approaches to extract insights from various customer touchpoints. These touchpoints include sources such as call center queries and online forums. This definition comes from the BBC Global Experience Language.

What Does a UX Writer Do in Conversation Mining?

A UX writer engaging in conversation mining initiates dialogues across different platforms, such as customer hotlines, product reviews, blog posts, social media, and forums. These discussions primarily revolve around the brand and its products but can also extend to general conversations related to the product's domain.

Goals of Conversation Mining

The objectives of conversation mining encompass:

- Understanding user preferences and dislikes about a brand, product, or service.
- Identifying potential usability issues with products.
- Uncovering additional user information needs.
- Gaining insights into user vocabulary, including how they express themselves and their language choices.

How Does Conversation Mining Work?

Here's a breakdown of the process:

1. Set Your Research Objective: Clearly define what you want to achieve, whether it's establishing a brand voice or understanding user sentiments about a service.
2. Determine Research Questions: Formulate specific questions aligned with your research objective. For instance, if exploring

brand voice, questions could revolve around positive and negative aspects mentioned by users.

3. Define Sources/Channels: Decide where to ask your research questions, selecting platforms such as forums and social media.

4. Collect Conversational Raw Materials: Gather information provided by users in various forms like lists, documents, audio, videos, texts, and screenshots.

5. Prepare and Analyze Data: Organize the collected data, removing redundancy and highlighting key patterns or noteworthy information.

6. Present Results: Share your findings with stakeholders or relevant parties who can benefit from the insights.

Examples of Conversation Mining Use:

Writing Copy for an Insurance Company Website: Consult the customer service team to uncover frequently asked questions and common concerns from customers.

Creating Copy for a Diabetes Tracking App: Utilize conversation mining to identify relevant symptoms by exploring self-reports on forums and social media platforms.

Importance of Conversation Mining in UX Writing

Conversation mining is crucial for UX writing because it:

- Provides direct access to target audiences.
- Supplies specific user needs, revealing knowledge gaps and misunderstandings.

- Informs about the vocabulary and terms commonly used by the target audience.

Strengths and Weaknesses of Conversation Mining

Strengths:

- Offers deep insights into the natural language of the target audience.
- Provides glimpses into customers' personal lives.
- Allows understanding of user likes and dislikes.
- Platforms are easily accessible and cost-effective.

Weaknesses:

- Data may be complex, excessive, and ambiguous.
- Authenticity of the data may be questioned.
- Language-based data analysis expertise may be needed.
- Choice of platforms or channels is critical for representative data.

Mitigating Weaknesses:

- Choose sources wisely.
- Distinguish valuable data from irrelevant or spam content.
- Acquire knowledge of statistics and data analysis tools.
- Complement conversation mining with other user research methods.

Tools for Conversation Mining: Several social media listening and tracking tools can aid in conversation mining:

1. Sprout Social

2. Buffer

3. Agorapulse

4. HubSpot Social Media Management Software

5. Falcon.io

6. Mention

7. Hootsuite

8. TweetReach

9. Awario

10. Buzzsumo

The focus of conversation mining for a UX writer extends beyond what target audiences are discussing to how they are discussing it. While valuable, conversation mining should complement other data gathered through various user research methods.

Understanding Target Group Observation

According to Channel Play, target group observation is a qualitative research method where subjects are discreetly observed and analyzed in their natural and real-world environments. Unlike conversation mining, target group observation goes beyond simply reading or hearing what your audience thinks or does. It involves the added dimension of watching their behavior unfold in real-life situations. The observation methods can take various forms, including covert and overt observations.

Types of Observations

Covert Observations: Researchers don't disclose their identity, blending into the crowd or observing from a distance.

Overt Observations: Researchers reveal themselves to the target audience, and subjects are aware of their presence.

Goals of Target Group Observation

- Detecting behavioral patterns.
- Identifying orientation patterns.
- Gaining insights into people's preferences.
- Understanding factors influencing behavior.
- Learning about the audience's choice of words.
- Observing how people actually use a product.

How Target Group Observation Works

Clearly define what you aim to achieve, then identify specific questions aligned with your research objectives. Develop a structured template for collecting data and specify the environment for your observation. Next stage is to execute your observation strategy and collect information systematically and analyze the data. Lastly, communicate your findings to your team.

Importance of Target Group Observation

Observations are indispensable for anyone involved in creating digital products. While direct interviews provide valuable insights, observations, especially covert ones, unveil aspects that the audience might not explicitly share because they may not be aware of them. This method also reveals the vocabulary and terms users use when discussing the product.

Strengths and Weaknesses of Target Group Observation

Strengths:

- Authentic insights.
- No subject cooperation is necessary.
- Flexibility allows for real-time adjustments.
- Researchers develop a deeper understanding of user needs.

Weaknesses:

- May consume time and resources.
- Limited observation scope.
- Subjective data documentation.
- Challenging data consolidation.
- Difficulty in explaining subconscious observations.

Considerations for Effective Target Group Observation

1. Involve researchers early in the project.
2. Stay attentive and be prepared to adapt swiftly.
3. Seek permission for research activities.
4. Maintain respect and politeness toward subjects.
5. Include a second or third observer for unbiased opinions.

In essence, target group observation provides a nuanced understanding of user behavior, offering authentic insights that can significantly impact UX writing and product development.

Focus Groups and How They Work

Focus groups are dynamic and interactive discussions involving a small group of participants, usually 6 to 10 individuals, brought together to express their opinions, experiences, and perceptions about a specific topic or product. This qualitative research method encourages participants to share their thoughts openly, fostering valuable insights that may not surface through individual interviews or surveys.

Goals of a Focus Group

- Exploration of Perceptions: Understand how participants perceive a product or concept.
- In-depth Understanding: Delve into participants' experiences and feelings related to the discussed topic.
- Idea Generation: Generate creative ideas and solutions through group interaction.
- Collective Insights: Uncover collective opinions and consensus within the group.
- Feedback Collection: Gather feedback on specific features, designs, or concepts.

How Focus Groups Work

1. **Planning:** Define the research objectives and select participants based on relevant criteria.
2. **Moderation:** A skilled moderator guides the discussion, ensuring all participants have an opportunity to share their perspectives.
3. **Interaction:** Participants engage in open conversations, responding to questions posed by the moderator and sharing their experiences.
4. **Observation:** Researchers observe participants' body language, expressions, and group dynamics to glean additional insights.
5. **Analysis:** Recorded sessions are analyzed to identify patterns, common themes, and significant insights.

6. **Reporting:** The findings are compiled into a comprehensive report, providing actionable recommendations for product development.

Tabular List of Questions

Type of Question	Example
Open-ended Questions	"What are your initial thoughts about the product?"
	"Can you describe a situation where you might use it?"
	"How do you feel about the design of the interface?"
Closed-ended Questions	"On a scale of 1 to 10, how likely are you to recommend this product?"
	"Which feature do you find most appealing, A or B?"
	"Do you currently use a similar product? Yes/No"
Follow-up Questions	"Can you elaborate more on your experience with that particular feature?"

Type of Question	Example
	"You mentioned a concern earlier; can you provide more details?"
	"How do you think this product compares to others you've used in the past?"

Criteria for Focus Group Questions

Questions should be clear and easily understandable by participants. Ensure questions directly relate to the research objectives and topic. Avoid leading or biased questions to maintain objectivity. Another essential criteria is to Incorporate open-ended questions to encourage diverse responses. Also, questions should be engaging, sparking thoughtful responses. Lastly, the writer should structure questions in a logical sequence to facilitate a smooth flow of discussion. Remember, the art of crafting focus group questions lies in promoting candid conversation, fostering genuine insights, and ultimately contributing to informed product development decisions.

User Interviews in Research

User interviews are one-on-one conversations between a researcher and a user, designed to gather detailed insights into the user's experiences, preferences, and needs. This qualitative research method aims to uncover valuable information that informs the design and improvement of products or services.

Goals of User Interviews

When a UX writer conducts an interview, the aim is to gain a deep understanding of users' thoughts, feelings, and experiences. Another reason is to uncover any challenges or frustrations users may encounter with a product or service. During this process the UX writer will gather feedback on specific features, designs, or functionalities. This is done in order to confirm if the design aligns with user expectations and requirements. It also encourages users to provide suggestions and ideas for enhancing the user experience.

How User Interviews Work

- **Preparation**: Define interview goals, select participants, and develop a list of questions.
- **Engagement:** The interviewer establishes rapport, creating a comfortable atmosphere for open conversation.
- **Questioning:** Open-ended and probing questions are posed to encourage detailed responses.
- **Active Listening**: The interviewer actively listens to the user's responses, probing further when necessary.
- **Observation:** Non-verbal cues and reactions are noted to complement the verbal responses.
- **Analysis:** Recorded interviews are analyzed to identify patterns, trends, and actionable insights.
- **Reporting:** The findings are compiled into a report, providing recommendations for UX improvement.

Importance of Interviews for UX Writing

User interviews are crucial for UX writing because they provide direct access to the user's perspective, language, and preferences. They offer a nuanced understanding that goes beyond quantitative data, allowing UX writers to tailor their content to meet user needs effectively.

Tabular Form of Questions:

Type of Question	Example
Open-ended Question	"Can you tell me about your experience using our product?"
Probing Questions	"What specific features did you find most useful or frustrating?"
	"How did you feel when interacting with the interface?"
	"Can you describe a situation where the product exceeded your expectations?"
	"Are there any aspects of the product that you find confusing or unclear?"
Follow-up	"You mentioned finding the interface confusing; can

Type of Question	Example
Questions	you provide more details?"
	"Could you elaborate on the challenges you faced with the specific feature?"
	"Tell me more about your expectations when using similar products."
	"How do you think the product could better meet your needs?"

Criteria for Questions

1. Ensure questions are phrased in a friendly and clear manner.
2. Encourage participants to share their thoughts openly by using conversational language.
3. Probing questions should dive deeper into specific aspects, avoiding superficial responses.
4. Ask questions in different ways to solicit varied perspectives and insights.
5. Demonstrate empathy in your questioning, showing genuine interest in the user's experiences.

User interviews provide a rich source of qualitative data that is invaluable for UX writers, allowing them to craft content that resonates with the target audience and enhances the overall user experience.

Method of Validating User Research & Testing for UX Writing

Validating user research, also known as Evaluative research, is a fundamental step in testing written content to ensure it meets users' needs. Whether it's for an entire product, a feature, or a specific element, this method helps guarantee that the written material is top-notch and serves users effectively.

Interaction Design Foundation defines validating user research as a systematic study of target users, focusing on their needs and pain points. The goal is to provide writers with sharp insights for crafting the best possible copy.

Exploratory vs. Validating Research

In a nutshell, Exploratory Research examines subjects before building a product's feature to gain deeper insights while Validating Research Involves collecting and analyzing data to test and validate hypotheses and concepts within an existing product.

Variety of Validating User Research Methods

1. A/B Testing
2. Card sorting
3. Close testing
4. Comprehensive surveys
5. Highlighter testing

6. Search team Analysis
7. Usability tests

Differences between Exploratory research and Validating Research	
Exploratory	**Validating**
Product Discovery for a New Social Media App: A tech company plans to launch a new social media app. Before designing features, they conduct exploratory research to understand users' social media habits, preferences, and pain points. They may use methods like in-depth interviews and online surveys to explore potential user needs and expectations.	**A/B Testing Email Copy for Higher Engagement:** An e-commerce company wants to improve email engagement. They create two versions of an email with different copy approaches. Through A/B testing, they send each version to a segment of their audience and analyze metrics such as open rates and click-through rates. The version that performs better is validated for broader use.
Understanding Traveler Preferences for a Booking Platform: A travel booking platform is considering adding a new feature to enhance user experience. Before implementation, the company conducts exploratory research to understand traveler preferences. They may organize focus group discussions or user	**Usability Testing for a Mobile Banking App Feature:** A banking app wants to introduce a new feature allowing users to easily transfer money between accounts. Before the full launch, they conduct usability testing with a group of users. Participants are asked to perform specific tasks using the new feature, and their interactions are

interviews to explore what features would make the booking process more convenient and enjoyable for users.	observed. The testing validates whether the feature is user-friendly and effective.
Market Research for a Fitness Wearable: A company planning to launch a new fitness wearable engages in exploratory research to understand the market landscape. They may analyze competitor products, conduct interviews with potential users, and explore current trends in health and fitness. This helps them identify gaps in the market and potential areas for innovation.	**Close Testing for Ad Copy Effectiveness:** An online advertising campaign is being developed, and different copies are drafted. To validate the most effective ad copy, the team conducts close testing. Users are shown various ad versions, and their feedback is collected through surveys or interviews. This helps the team choose the copy that resonates best with the target audience.

Why Validating User Research is Vital for UX Writing

- Ensures copy quality by testing copy with real users to guarantee effectiveness and clarity
- Assesses voice and tone perception and helps to understands how users perceive the writing style.
- Demonstrates impact to stakeholders by showing stakeholders the real impact of writing decisions
- Provides clarity for copy improvement when users contribute ideas to enhance copy relatability

- Helps to gains general insights into the target audience preference
- Improves writing skills and identifies personal biases

Preparing for Validating User Research

1. **Define Research Goals:** Align with company Key Performance Indicators (KPIs) and UX writing quality criteria.
2. **Company KPIs Examples:** Companies should target certain measurable KPIs to decide if their research is successful. These KPIs include: Increase signups, user duration, reduce drop-off rates, and increase completed purchases.
3. **UX Writing Quality Criteria:** Necessary, Concise, Clear, Useful, Conversational, Branded.
4. **Ask UX Writing Criteria Questions**: The research questions should be centered on answering these 3 primary questions: Do users understand the copy? Does it help them overcome hurdles? Does it reflect our brand?
5. **General Content Criteria:** Content must pass the following test to provide the best user experience. Readability, Usability, Comprehension, Navigability, Accessibility, Searchability
6. **Readability Scores:** This is a score of how easily users can read and understand your texts or writing. These can be checked with the following tools: Gunning Fog, Flesh Kincaid Index, SMOG Index, Dale-Call Readability Formula.
7. **Define Copy Element Purpose:** Understand the intended purpose of each text element.
8. **Organize Research Results:** Create structured folders for questionnaires and collected data.
9. **Educate Yourself:** Explore various user research methods to enhance understanding.

10. **Consider Data Privacy Rules:** Adhere to data privacy rules, especially for exploratory research.
11. **Plan Incentives:** If needed, plan incentives for participants that will be involved in the research and testing to ensure engagement
12. **Time and Cost Scope:** Plan the duration and cost scope of the study.
13. **Start Your Research Journey**: Once prepared, begin the validating user research journey with selected methods and approaches.

Impact of Search Term Analysis

Search term analysis, often referred to as keyword analysis, is a research method that involves evaluating the terms and phrases users employ when conducting searches, particularly on search engines like Google. The goal is to understand user intent, preferences, and the language they use, aiding in optimizing content for search engine visibility and relevance.

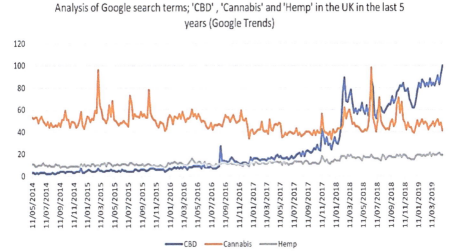

Analysis of Google search terms; 'CBD', 'Cannabis' and 'Hemp' in the UK in the last 5 years (Google Trends)

Examples of Search Term Analysis include:

E-commerce Platform:

An e-commerce platform aims to enhance its product pages for better search visibility. Through search term analysis, the team identifies commonly used terms related to their products, ensuring these terms are strategically incorporated into product descriptions, titles, and metadata.

Blog Content Strategy:

A blogger wants to create content that resonates with their audience. By analyzing search terms related to their niche, they uncover trending topics and specific phrases frequently searched by their target audience. This guides content creation for maximum relevance and organic traffic.

Local Business Optimization:

A local restaurant wishes to improve its online presence. Through search term analysis, they identify location-specific keywords potential customers use when searching for restaurants. The business then optimizes its website and online profiles with these keywords to appear in relevant local searches.

Goal of Search Term Analysis

The primary goal of search term analysis is to gain insights into the language users use when searching for information online. This research method aims to understand user intent, refine content to match user expectations, and optimize for search engines. Ultimately, the goal is to enhance visibility, increase organic traffic, and deliver content that meets user needs.

How to Conduct Search Term Analysis

Conducting a search term analysis involves several key steps:

Identify Your Audience

Clearly define your target audience to tailor the analysis to the language and preferences of your specific user demographic.

Brainstorm Seed Keywords

Begin with a list of seed keywords relevant to your content or business. These are general terms that broadly represent your offerings.

Use Keyword Research Tools

Leverage keyword research tools like Google Keyword Planner, SEMrush, or Ahrefs to explore related keywords, search volumes, and competition. These tools provide valuable insights into what terms users commonly search for.

Analyze User Intent

Consider the intent behind each keyword. Are users looking for information, making a purchase, or seeking specific services? Understanding intent helps tailor content appropriately.

Long-Tail Keyword Exploration

Look beyond broad terms and explore long-tail keywords – more specific phrases that users might search for. These can often capture users with a clearer intent.

Competitor Analysis

Analyze the keywords your competitors are targeting. Identify gaps or areas where you can differentiate your content.

User Surveys and Feedback

Directly engage with your audience through surveys or feedback forms to understand the terms they use and their preferences. Real user input provides invaluable insights.

Create a Final Keyword List

Compile a comprehensive list of keywords relevant to your content or business. Prioritize based on relevance, search volume, and competition.

Optimize Content

Implement the identified keywords strategically in your content, titles, meta descriptions, and other relevant areas. Ensure a natural and user-friendly integration.

Monitor and Iterate

Regularly review and update your keyword strategy based on shifts in user behavior, industry trends, and changes in search engine algorithms.

Why Search Term Analysis is Important for UX Writing

User-Centric Content: By understanding the language users use, UX writers can create content that resonates with their audience, ensuring a user-centric approach.

Enhanced Visibility: Incorporating relevant search terms increases the likelihood of content appearing in search results, enhancing visibility and attracting organic traffic.

Improved User Experience: Users find what they're looking for more easily when content is optimized for their commonly used terms, leading to an improved overall user experience.

Tailored Messaging: Search term analysis provides insights into user intent, allowing UX writers to tailor messaging to align with the specific needs and expectations of the audience.

Strategic Content Creation: Writers can strategically create content around trending or high-volume keywords, ensuring their work aligns with what users are actively searching for.

Competitive Edge: By staying informed about competitor keyword strategies, UX writers can identify opportunities to differentiate their content and gain a competitive edge.

Pros and Cons of Using Search Term Analysis

Pros:

- Enables precise content creation aligned with user expectations and interests.
- Enhances search engine optimization, increasing the likelihood of content ranking higher in search results.
- Offers valuable insights into user preferences, language, and intent.
- Informs strategic decisions in content creation, marketing, and overall business strategy.
- Helps allocate resources efficiently by focusing efforts on keywords with high relevance and potential.

Cons:

- Overemphasis on keywords may lead to unnatural-sounding content, affecting the overall user experience.
- Search engine algorithms evolve, impacting the effectiveness of previously identified keywords.

- Focus on keywords may overlook broader contextual aspects that contribute to user engagement.
- Reliance on keyword research tools may limit creativity and miss nuances that tools might not capture.
- High competition for certain keywords may make it challenging to achieve and maintain top search rankings.

.

A/B Testing Method

A/B testing, also known as split testing, is a method of comparing two versions (A and B) of a webpage, app, or any user interface to determine which performs better. It involves presenting these variations to different groups of users simultaneously and analyzing their responses to identify the more effective version.

CTA BUTTON COLOR

Version A

Hi!

We've just launched a new feature - Email Scheduling.

Now you can:
- schedule according to the recipient's time zone
- choose the days on which no emails will be sent
- set hours between which emails will be delivered for maximum engagement
- plus, set up follow-up reminders

Hope you enjoy it!
Test out the new feature by clicking the button below.

TRY NOW

Version B

Hi!

We've just launched a new feature - Email Scheduling.

Now you can:
- schedule according to the recipient's time zone
- choose the days on which no emails will be sent
- set hours between which emails will be delivered for maximum engagement
- plus, set up follow-up reminders

Hope you enjoy it!
Test out the new feature by clicking the button below.

TRY NOW

Click-through rate results

38% vs 25%

Version A   Version B

Here are a few examples of what A/B Testing is like:

E-commerce Checkout Process:

An online retailer wants to improve the checkout process to reduce cart abandonment. Version A has a multi-step checkout, while Version B features a simplified single-step process. The goal is to determine which version leads to higher conversion rates and reduced cart abandonment.

Call-to-Action Button Design:

A subscription-based service aims to increase sign-ups through its website. Version A showcases a green call-to-action button, while Version B uses a blue button. The goal is to identify the button color that results in more user sign-ups.

Email Marketing Subject Lines:

A marketing team wants to optimize email open rates for a promotional campaign. Version A includes a straightforward subject line, while Version B uses a curiosity-inducing subject line. The goal here is to determine which subject line leads to higher email open rates.

Goal of A/B Testing:

The primary goal of A/B testing is to make informed decisions by comparing variations and understanding their impact on user behavior. Whether it's increasing conversion rates, improving engagement, or refining user interactions, A/B testing provides quantitative insights into what resonates best with the audience.

What to Test in A/B Testing

1. **CTA Elements:** Test variations in call-to-action (CTA) buttons, such as color, size, text, and placement.
2. **Page Layout and Design:** Experiment with different layouts, color schemes, and visual elements to assess their impact on user engagement.
3. **Content and Messaging:** Test variations in headlines, product descriptions, and overall messaging to understand what captures user attention.
4. **Forms and Input Fields:** Optimize forms by testing different input field arrangements, label placements, and overall form complexity.
5. **Navigation and User Flow**: Experiment with navigation menus and user flow to identify the most intuitive and user-friendly design.
6. **Images and Multimedia:** Test different images, videos, or other multimedia elements to gauge their impact on user engagement.
7. **Pricing and Promotions**: Assess the effectiveness of different pricing models, discount structures, or promotional offers.

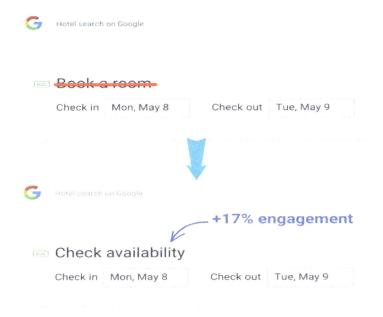

How to Effectively Use A/B Testing

- **Define Clear Objectives:** Clearly outline the specific goals you aim to achieve with the A/B test, such as increased conversions, higher engagement, or reduced bounce rates.
- **Choose Significant Variables:** Select variables that have a substantial impact on user behavior and are feasible to test within the given timeframe.
- **Randomized Assignment:** Ensure that users are randomly assigned to either Version A or Version B to eliminate bias and ensure accurate results.

- **Sufficient Sample Size:** Collect data from a sufficiently large sample size to ensure statistical significance and reliability of the results.
- **Monitor User Behavior Metrics:** Track relevant metrics, such as conversion rates, click-through rates, or time spent on page, to assess the performance of each variation.
- **Statistical Analysis:** Use statistical analysis to determine if the observed differences between versions are statistically significant or if they could be due to random chance.
- **Iterate and Learn:** Based on the results, iterate and implement the changes that lead to improved outcomes. Continuously learn from each A/B test to refine future experiments.
- **Consider User Segmentation**: Segment your audience based on relevant characteristics, such as demographics or user behavior, to uncover insights specific to different user groups.

Why A/B Testing is Important for UX Writing

A/B testing provides concrete data on user preferences, allowing UX writers to make informed decisions backed by real user behavior. Writers can experiment with different headlines, copy variations, and messaging styles to identify what resonates best with the target audience.

Testing different CTA button texts or styles helps writers understand how to craft compelling calls to action that encourage user interaction. Experimenting with content layout, font styles, and readability aspects helps writers refine the clarity and presentation of written content.

A/B testing allows writers to adapt content to user preferences, ensuring that the language and tone align with what resonates most with the audience.

Pros and Cons of A/B Testing

Pros:

- Informed decision-making based on concrete data rather than assumptions or intuition.
- A/B testing fosters a culture of continuous improvement by iterating based on user feedback.
- Results are quantifiable, allowing for clear comparisons between different versions.
- Provides an objective evaluation of the effectiveness of design, content, or features
- Testing mitigates the risk of implementing changes without understanding their impact.

Cons:

- A/B testing can be resource-intensive, requiring time, technology, and a significant user base for meaningful results.
- A/B testing may not capture the full complexity of user interactions and experiences, especially in intricate user journeys.
- Biases can affect results if not accounted for, such as selection bias or variations in user behavior over time.
- A/B testing may emphasize short-term gains, potentially overlooking long-term impacts on user behavior.
- Interpreting results requires a good understanding of statistical analysis, and misinterpretations can lead to misguided decisions.

Conducting A Comprehension Survey

A comprehensive survey, in the context of UX writing, refers to a methodical and thorough examination of users' understanding and interpretation of written content within a digital product. This type of survey aims to gather detailed insights into how well users comprehend the information presented to them, assessing factors such as clarity, readability, and overall user understanding. Through a combination of carefully crafted questions, rating scales, and open-ended inquiries, comprehensive surveys provide both quantitative and qualitative data to inform UX writers about the effectiveness of their written content and guide iterative improvements for an enhanced user experience.

Here are examples of Comprehension Surveys

"How easily were you able to find the information you were looking for on our website?"

"Please describe your understanding of the new feature introduced in the latest app update."

"Did you find the labels for each field in the registration form clear and easy to understand?"

"What is your interpretation of the message displayed when an error occurs during the login process?"

Goal of Comprehension Surveys

The primary goal of comprehension surveys in UX writing is to ensure that written content is clear, easily understood, and aligns with the user's mental model. By assessing comprehension, UX writers can identify areas for improvement, refine messaging, and enhance the overall user experience. Here aree some steps to Creating a Comprehension Survey:

- **Define Survey Objectives:** Clearly outline the goals of the comprehension survey, specifying what aspects of comprehension you aim to evaluate.
- **Identify Target Audience:** Determine the demographic or user segment for whom the content is intended, ensuring that the survey reflects the perspectives of the target audience.
- **Select Survey Methodology:** Choose the survey format, whether it's a post-interaction survey, in-app prompt, or email questionnaire, based on the context of user interaction.
- **Develop Clear Questions:** Craft survey questions that directly address the aspects of comprehension you want to assess. Use clear and concise language to avoid ambiguity.
- **Include Open-Ended Questions:** Incorporate open-ended questions to encourage users to provide detailed feedback and insights into their understanding.
- **Utilize Rating Scales:** Implement rating scales or Likert scales to gather quantitative data on the user's perception of clarity, with options ranging from "Strongly Disagree" to "Strongly Agree."
- **Pilot Test the Survey:** Conduct a pilot test with a small group of users to identify any issues with question clarity, survey flow, or potential bias.

- **Iterate Based on Feedback:** Iterate the survey based on feedback from the pilot test, ensuring that questions are unbiased, easy to comprehend, and align with the survey objectives.
- **Distribute the Survey:** Deploy the survey to the target audience, using the chosen methodology, and collect responses for analysis.
- **Analyze Results:** Analyze survey responses to identify patterns, trends, and areas where users may face challenges in comprehension.
- **Generate Actionable Insights:** Translate survey findings into actionable insights, informing UX writing improvements, content adjustments, or interface modifications.

Why is Comprehension Survey Important for UX Writing

1. Comprehension surveys ensure that users can easily understand and navigate through digital interfaces, contributing to a positive user experience.
2. By assessing comprehension, UX writers can align written content with user expectations, reducing confusion and frustration.
3. Continuous comprehension surveys guide iterative improvements, allowing UX writers to refine content based on user feedback and evolving user needs.
4. Effective communication is central to UX writing. Comprehension surveys help optimize communication by tailoring messaging to resonate with the target audience.
5. Insights from comprehension surveys inform broader content strategies, ensuring that written content aligns with organizational goals and user preferences.

Pros and Cons of Comprehension Surveys

Pros:

- Surveys prioritize user feedback, enabling targeted improvements that directly address user comprehension challenges.
- Comprehension surveys offer a blend of quantitative data (ratings) and qualitative data (open-ended responses), providing a comprehensive understanding.
- The iterative nature of comprehension surveys supports ongoing optimization, allowing for continuous enhancement of written content.
- Clear and comprehensible content prevents user frustration, leading to higher satisfaction and retention rates.
- Surveys provide an objective evaluation of content clarity, reducing subjectivity in assessing user comprehension.

Cons:

- Users may provide biased responses based on their own interpretations, and cultural or linguistic factors can influence feedback.
- Surveys rely on users' interpretations, which may not fully capture the intended message or account for diverse perspectives.
- The effectiveness of comprehension surveys depends on the clarity and neutrality of survey questions, which may introduce unintentional biases.
- Measuring comprehension is complex, and survey responses may not always accurately reflect the user's actual understanding.
- Designing, deploying, and analyzing comprehension surveys can be resource and time-intensive, especially for frequent iterations.

Card Sorting Method

Card sorting, within UX writing, is a user-centered research method used to understand how individuals organize and categorize information. In this method, participants are presented with a set of cards, each representing a piece of content, and are tasked with organizing them into groups that make sense to them. This process provides valuable insights into users' mental models, helping UX writers structure information in a way that aligns with user expectations.

Here are a few examples of Card Sorting:

Website Navigation: Participants sort cards representing different website sections to help designers understand how users expect information to be grouped for easy navigation.

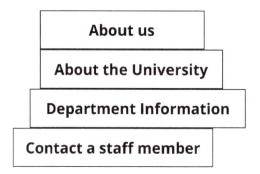

Product Feature Organization: Users categorize cards representing various features in a product to guide UX writers in creating intuitive interfaces and user flows.

Content Hierarchy: Cards with content snippets are sorted to unveil users' preferences for content hierarchy, assisting writers in prioritizing information.

Menu Structure: Testing the arrangement of menu items by having participants sort cards helps optimize menu structures for enhanced user experience.

How Card Sorting Works

Preparation:

- Identify the content or information you want insights on.
- Create cards, each representing a distinct piece of content.
- Select participants representing your target audience.

Card Sorting Sessions:

- Participants are given the set of cards and asked to organize them into groups that make sense to them.
- Participants can also label the groups they create.

Data Collection:

- Gather data on how participants categorize the cards and any labels they assign to the groups.

Analysis:

- Analyze the collected data to identify patterns, common groupings, and potential areas of confusion.

Iterative Refinement:

- Use insights from card sorting to iteratively refine the information architecture, content structure, and navigation elements.

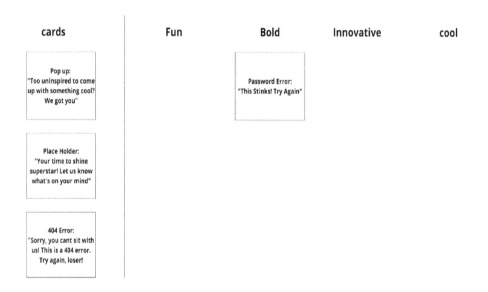

The Goal of Card Sorting

The primary goal of card sorting is to uncover how users naturally categorize and organize information. By understanding users' mental models, UX writers can structure content in a way that resonates with the audience, improving overall usability and user satisfaction.

Types of Card Sorting Methods

Open Card Sorting:

- Participants create their own categories without predefined labels.
- Provides insights into how users conceptualize and group information.

Closed Card Sorting:

- Participants organize cards into predefined categories.
- Useful for validating existing information architectures and evaluating user understanding of predetermined structures.

Hybrid Card Sorting:

- Combines elements of both open and closed card sorting.
- Participants create their own categories but can choose from predefined labels if needed.

Why Card Sorting is Important in UX Writing

1. **User-Centric Content Organization:** Card sorting ensures that content is organized in a way that aligns with users' mental models, making information easily accessible.
2. **Improved Information Architecture:** Insights from card sorting guide the development of effective information architectures, enhancing the overall structure of digital products.
3. **Enhanced Navigation:** By understanding how users expect information to be grouped, UX writers can optimize navigation elements for a smoother user experience.
4. **Informed Content Hierarchy:** Card sorting helps determine the priority and hierarchy of content, allowing writers to emphasize crucial information.

5. **Reduced Cognitive Load:** A well-organized structure, informed by card sorting, reduces cognitive load on users, leading to a more enjoyable and efficient interaction.

Pros and Cons of Card Sorting

Pros:

- Provides direct insights into how users think about and organize content.
- Guides the development of effective and user-friendly information architectures.
- Helps align content strategy with user expectations and preferences.
- Supports iterative refinement of content organization based on user feedback.
- Generally a cost-effective method for gathering valuable user insights.

Cons:

- Relies on users' subjective perspectives, which may not cover all potential scenarios.
- Users may interpret cards differently, leading to ambiguity in sorting.
- The effectiveness of results may be influenced by the size and diversity of the participant pool.

- The artificial setting of card sorting may not fully replicate real-world usage scenarios.

Tools for Effective Card Sorting

1. OptimalSort: Offers both online and in-person card sorting tools with robust analytics.
2. UserZoom: Provides card sorting capabilities along with other UX research tools.
3. Treejack: Focuses on information architecture testing, including card sorting.
4. Miro: Collaborative online whiteboard platform suitable for remote card sorting sessions.
5. UsabilityHub: Offers a range of usability testing tools, including card sorting.

Cloze Testing Technique

According to Wikipedia, Cloze testing is a method employed in UX writing to assess the comprehensibility and effectiveness of written content, particularly in user interfaces. The test involves removing specific words from a passage or text and asking participants to fill in the blanks with what they believe fits contextually. This approach evaluates users' understanding, language proficiency, and the clarity of the provided content.

How Cloze Testing Works

1. **Preparation:** Select a passage or piece of content that aligns with the objectives of the test. Identify the words to be removed, ensuring they are strategically chosen to gauge user comprehension.
2. **Creating the Test:** Remove the chosen words, leaving blanks or spaces in their place and ensure that the context remains coherent even with the removed words.
3. **Participant Interaction:** Participants are presented with the cloze test and are asked to fill in the blanks with words they believe fit the context.
4. **Data Collection:** Collect responses from participants, noting the words they choose to fill in the blanks.
5. **Analysis:** Analyze the completed cloze tests to identify patterns, common misunderstandings, and areas where users may struggle.
6. **Iterative Refinement:** Use insights from the cloze test to iteratively refine the content, focusing on improving clarity and user understanding.

Cloze Test Samples

Original Text: "Effective communication is crucial in ensuring users understand the functionality and purpose of a digital product. Clear and concise language helps users navigate through interfaces with ease."

Cloze Test: "Effective communication is crucial in ensuring users _____ the functionality and purpose of a digital _____. Clear and concise language helps users navigate _____ interfaces with ease."

Types of Cloze Tests

1. **Deletion Cloze Test:** In this traditional form, every nth word is systematically removed, leaving gaps for participants to fill.
2. **Multiple-Choice Cloze Test:** Participants are provided with a set of options for each blank, requiring them to select the most appropriate word.
3. **Open-Ended Cloze Test:** Similar to the deletion cloze test, but participants are not provided with a list of options, requiring them to generate their own responses.

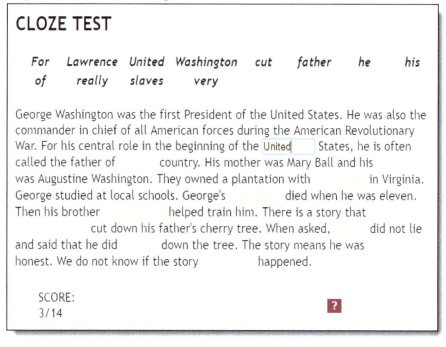

CLOZE TEST

| For | Lawrence | United | Washington | cut | father | he | his |
| of | really | slaves | very |

George Washington was the first President of the United States. He was also the commander in chief of all American forces during the American Revolutionary War. For his central role in the beginning of the United States, he is often called the father of   country. His mother was Mary Ball and his   was Augustine Washington. They owned a plantation with   in Virginia. George studied at local schools. George's   died when he was eleven. Then his brother   helped train him. There is a story that   cut down his father's cherry tree. When asked,   did not lie and said that he did   down the tree. The story means he was honest. We do not know if the story   happened.

SCORE:
3/14

Importance of Cloze Testing in UX Writing

- Cloze testing evaluates how well users comprehend written content, helping UX writers gauge the effectiveness of their communication.
- Ambiguities in language can lead to varied interpretations. Cloze testing highlights areas where users may interpret content differently than intended.
- By examining user responses, UX writers can identify unclear or confusing passages and make necessary adjustments to enhance clarity.
- Cloze testing indirectly assesses users' language proficiency and their familiarity with the terminology used in the content.
- Insights from cloze testing guide the use of user-centric language, ensuring that written content aligns with the language and understanding of the target audience.

Tools for Cloze Testing

1. Google Forms
2. SurveyMonkey
3. Typeform
4. Microsoft Forms
5. Qualtrics

Pros and Cons of Cloze Testing

Pros:

- **Quick Assessment:** Cloze tests provide a relatively quick way to assess user comprehension of specific content.

- **Identifies Ambiguities:** Ambiguous or confusing language is revealed through participant responses, enabling targeted improvements.
- **Objective Evaluation:** Results are objective, allowing for clear insights into areas where users may struggle to understand.
- **Iterative Improvement:** The iterative nature of cloze testing allows for continuous refinement of content based on user feedback.

Cons:

- **Limited Context:** Cloze tests focus on specific passages, potentially overlooking the broader context in which the content exists.
- **Sensitivity to Word Choice:** The effectiveness of cloze testing can be sensitive to the choice of words removed, influencing user responses.
- **Surface-Level Assessment:** While effective for assessing surface-level comprehension, cloze tests may not capture deeper nuances of user understanding.

Highlighter Testing for Quantitative Research

Highlighter testing is a method used in UX writing to assess user interactions with written content by having them highlight or mark specific elements. This method aims to uncover user preferences, comprehension levels, and areas of interest within a given text. By observing how users interact with content through highlighting, UX writers can glean valuable insights to enhance the user experience.

Most banks require Two-factor authentication to log in with a new device. Typically, users will add their email address and phone number for this process. You will proceed automatically in order to reach the dashboard after you approve your Log In request. In some cases, users will receive a physical device to authenticate themselves.

How Highlighter Testing Works

1. **Content Selection:** Choose a piece of content, such as a webpage, app screen, or document, that aligns with the goals of the test.
2. **Define Objectives:** Clearly outline the objectives of the highlighter test. What specific aspects of the content are you aiming to evaluate?
3. **Participant Instructions:** Instruct participants on the purpose of the test and guide them on how to use the highlighter tool. Emphasize that there are no right or wrong answers.
4. **Highlighting Process:** Participants engage with the content, using a digital or physical highlighter to mark elements they find interesting, confusing, relevant, or appealing.
5. **Collecting Data:** Gather data on the highlighted areas, patterns, and user preferences. This may involve observing participants in real-time or collecting feedback afterward.
6. **Analysis:** Analyze the collected data to identify common trends, areas of consensus, and any discrepancies in user highlighting patterns.

7. **Iterative Refinement:** Use insights from the highlighter test to iteratively refine the content, ensuring that it aligns more closely with user expectations and preferences.

Types of Highlighter Tests

1. **Content Emphasis Testing:** Participants highlight elements that draw their attention, indicating which parts of the content stand out to them.
2. **Confusion Identification:** Users mark areas where they feel confused or uncertain, helping identify potential pain points in the content.
3. **Relevance Assessment:** Participants highlight sections they find most relevant or valuable, providing insights into user priorities.
4. **Aesthetic Appeal Testing:** Users mark elements based on aesthetic preferences, helping gauge the visual appeal of the content.

Highlighting content

In this activity, mark words or phrases like this:

I can understand this

I am confused by this

Importance of Highlighter Testing in UX Writing

Highlighter testing emphasizes a user-centric approach, allowing writers to understand what elements resonate with the audience. Users can highlight confusing or unclear areas, helping UX writers pinpoint and address potential pain points. Insights from highlighter testing inform content optimization, ensuring that important information is readily accessible and engaging.

The test aids in evaluating the visual hierarchy of content, understanding which elements users prioritize when interacting with a page or screen. The iterative nature of highlighter testing enables continuous improvement, aligning content with user preferences over time.

Pros and Cons of Highlighter Testing

Pros:

- Highlighter testing provides visual, easily interpretable insights into user preferences and interactions.
- Conducted in real-time, this method allows for immediate observation of user behavior and preferences.
- Participants actively engage with the content, offering firsthand insights into their perceptions.
- The iterative nature of highlighter testing supports continuous refinement of content based on user feedback.

Cons:

- Interpretation of highlighted areas can be subjective, requiring careful analysis to derive meaningful insights.
- Highlighter testing is most effective for visual content and may be less applicable to purely textual information.
- Conducting highlighter tests may require resources for participant recruitment, observation, and data analysis.

- While qualitative, the method may offer limited quantitative data, making it essential to complement with other testing methods.

Complete Tools For UX Writing

UX writing involves a range of tools for writing, documentation, and research. Here's an extensive list categorizing tools based on their purposes in the UX writing process:

Writing Tools

Google Docs: Collaborative writing, drafting, and editing.

Microsoft Word: Creating and formatting documents.

Grammarly: Grammar and style checking, proofreading.

Hemingway Editor: Improving readability and clarity in writing.

ProWritingAid: Style, grammar, and readability analysis.

Collaboration and Communication Tools

Slack: Team communication and collaboration.

Microsoft Teams: Collaboration, file sharing, and communication.

Trello: Project management and task tracking.

Asana: Project planning and team collaboration.

Confluence: Collaborative documentation and knowledge sharing.

Research Tools

Google Search Console: Analyzing website performance in search results.

Google Analytics: Website and user behavior analytics.

Hotjar: Heatmaps, session recordings, and surveys for user behavior analysis.

UserTesting: Remote user testing and feedback gathering.

Optimal Workshop: Information architecture and usability testing.

User Research Tools

Dovetail: Qualitative data analysis and user research collaboration.

Lookback: Conducting remote user interviews and research.

UsabilityHub: Quick usability testing and feedback on designs.

Crazy Egg: Website heatmaps and A/B testing for user behavior analysis.

Miro: Collaborative online whiteboard for ideation and user journey mapping.

Content Creation and Design Tools

Figma: Collaborative design and prototyping.

Adobe XD: Design and prototyping for digital experiences.

Sketch: Vector-based design tool for user interfaces.

Canva: Graphic design tool for creating visuals and infographics.

Venngage: Infographic and visual content creation.

Content Management Systems (CMS)

WordPress: Blogging and content management.

Drupal: Open-source CMS for website development.

Contentful: Headless CMS for delivering content to multiple platforms.

Ghost: CMS for professional publishing and blogging.

HubSpot CMS: Content management and marketing automation.

SEO Tools

Moz: SEO analytics and keyword research.

SEMrush: SEO and competitive analysis.

Ahrefs: Backlink analysis and SEO toolset.

Yoast SEO: WordPress plugin for on-page SEO optimization.

Google Keyword Planner: Keyword research and planning.

Miscellaneous Tools

Loom: Video messaging and screen recording.

Zoom: Video conferencing for remote collaboration.

Snagit: Screen capture and image editing.

Mentimeter: Interactive presentations and audience engagement.

Axure RP: Prototyping and wireframing for interactive designs.

www.ingramcontent.com/pod-product-compliance
Lightning Source LLC
LaVergne TN
LVHW051736050326
832903LV00023B/955

* 9 7 9 8 8 6 9 6 9 1 1 3 2 *